Networks of Modernism

NETWORKS OF MODERNISM

Reorganizing American Narrative

WESLEY BEAL

University of Iowa Press, Iowa City

University of Iowa Press, Iowa City 52242

www.uiowapress.org
Printed in the United States of America

Design by Ashley Muehlbauer

The University of Iowa Press is a member of Green Press Initiative and is committed to preserving natural resources.

Printed on acid-free paper

Library of Congress Cataloging-in-Publication Data
Beal, Wesley.
Networks of modernism : reorganizing American narrative / by Wesley Beal.
pages cm
Includes bibliographical references and index.
ISBN 978-1-60938-351-0 (pbk)
ISBN 978-1-60938-352-7 (ebk)
1. Modernism (Literature)—United States. 2. American literature—20th century—History and criticism. I. Title.
PS228.M63B43 2015
810.9'112—dc23 2015004899

For Courtney and Reed and Wyatt

In the sky of liberty a new constellation will appear,
and its name will be America—many peoples, but one nation!

—Royal Dixon, *Americanization* (1916)

Contents

Acknowledgments

What are the acknowledgments if not the measure of one's own network of support and influence? As one records debts to mentors, colleagues, friends, and family, of course, pages like these diagram an array of nodal figures and their connective lines to the author. In my case, such debts exceed by far what I can enumerate here, so the following paragraphs should be understood as but an imperfect sketch of a large and still-expanding constellation.

I want first to thank my mentors. Susan Hegeman, Phil Wegner, Ed White, and Nora Alter were generous and illuminating in their support of this project during its earliest stages at the University of Florida. Even more humbling is their continued support for this work after I left the fold. This project is inestimably better for their guidance, and all of my subsequent work in writing and in the classroom bears the imprint of the enthusiasms and magnanimity they model for me. Other teachers—particularly David Leverenz, Jodi Schorb, and Malini Schueller at Florida, and before them Alex Vernon, Kevin Asman, and Rebecca Resinski at Hendrix College—provided me the contexts and tools that made this project thinkable.

I have also benefited from the generosity and genius of numerous colleagues. I received trenchant criticism from the Americanist dissertation circle that formed within the Marxist Reading Group at Florida. Jordan Dominy, Jim Liner, Mike Mayne, Patrick McHenry, and Christina Van Houten not only shared practical advice for revision and invaluable encouragement when I confronted stumbling blocks but also modeled what it means to be a good colleague and a good reader. Joel Winkelman, my close friend from Hendrix and fellow alumnus of the Brick House Institute, charitably counseled me on early drafts of the chapter on Randolph Bourne. Aaron Shaheen, a fellow Florida graduate, and Michael Simeone, a friend from Hendrix, shared advice on the revision process. At conferences extending from Victoria, British Columbia, to Falmouth, England, I tinkered with different elements of this project and benefited from audience members' suggestions to clarify my thinking, always returning home with new texts and arguments to work through. Those colleagues were often anonymous to me, but I especially thank Stacy Lavin and J. J. Butts for their work on our seminar at the Modernist Studies Association meeting in Victoria. The anonymous reviewers at the University of Iowa Press, *American Literary History*, and *Digital Humanities Quarterly* have shared indispensable criticism of argument and style without which this project would be direly impoverished. Carolyn Brown, my copyeditor at Iowa, saved the writing of this book from its writer. Lastly, Elisabeth Chretien, my editor at Iowa, provided valuable feedback on style, organization, and argument—and all the while suffered through my interminable questions about the publication process with matchless grace.

In addition to the generosity of my mentors and colleagues, I have also benefited from material support at several critical stages of this project. A Grinter Fellowship at Florida afforded me the time to focus on my writing, as did a Massey Dissertation Fellowship. The English department at Florida also generously supported my travel to conferences at Princeton University, the University of Texas, and University College Falmouth. Lyon College supported my travel to Victoria, and a junior faculty development grant from Dean Virginia Wray enabled me to study Randolph Bourne's papers at the Rare Book and Manuscript Library at Columbia University, which holds many of Bourne's papers as well as facsimiles of some letters that are held in the Alyse Gregory collection at the Beinecke Rare Book and Manuscript Library at Yale University. An excerpt from one letter from the Beinecke collection is reprinted by permission of Christopher Sinclair-Stevenson on behalf of the Estate of Alyse Gregory. I am also indebted to the institutional support of two journals. An earlier version of chapter 2 appeared as "The Form and Politics of Networks in Jean Toomer's *Cane*" in *American Literary History* 24.4 (2012) and appears by permission of Oxford University Press. An earlier version of chapter 4 appeared as "Network Narration in John Dos Passos's *U.S.A.* Trilogy" in *Digital Humanities Quarterly* 5.2 (2011).

In some cases, the support for this project was itself distributed, nodally related—in other words, with no central source or hierarchy underlying its organization. For example, when I found a note in Bourne's papers written in a French hand that was so illegible as to require a more intuitive reader, I posted a photograph of the note on Facebook and before I left the archives for the evening had compiled several responses into a strong working translation thanks to contributions from familiar people—particularly Ed White and Cathy Bordeau, my colleague from Lyon, and from Christina Van Houten, Fredrik Tydal, Isabelle Racine Tenace, and Carey Voss. I also received hints and fragments of translation from Sarah Peterson and Guylène Mortier Deasy, both of whom I had never met but who had seen the note shared across mutual friends' pages. Similarly, my visit to the Bourne papers was subsidized in part by Nina Rifkin and Marc Lerner, who let me crash on their futon even though we had never met before and had but one friend in common, Margaret LeJeune. Both cases gesture to the wide network of support that I have drawn on and also to the permutations of the distributed form that I study in this book.

And finally, to the ones with whom I have surrounded myself most, Courtney and Reed: I dedicate this book to you. Your love and support have sustained me, motivated me, and upheld the work of this book. In the wide distribution of our teachers, friends, and families, you will forever be the hub at the center of my world.

Networks of Modernism

Introduction

Networks and the Cultural Logic of Modernism

Like many events that signal a key break between periods, the publication of Gertrude Stein's *Three Lives* accrues its meaning largely after the fact of the event itself. Much of it composed as she sat for Pablo Picasso's portrait of her, *Three Lives* was published in 1909, three years after Stein completed it. Having failed to generate any interest with commercial publishers, Stein settled for a vanity press to print 1,500 copies of her short book, but even the president of the Grafton Press had reservations about accepting Stein's money. The story is often retold in Stein scholarship. Frederick Hitchcock insisted on sending a professional editor to work with Stein, writing: "My proof-readers report that there are some pretty bad slips in grammar, probably caused in the type-writing"; and even as the book was finally being printed, he chided: "I want to say frankly that I think you have written a very peculiar book and it will be a hard thing to make people take it seriously."[1] After a year, 73 copies of the book had sold; another 78 had been given to reviewers and friends.[2] By 1933, however, the same year that Stein published *The Autobiography of Alice B. Toklas*, the Modern Library edition of *Three Lives* would be a bestseller. Stein had become a celebrity, appearing on the cover of *Time* that year, and readers could now situate the book into a codified field of aesthetics that did not yet exist at the time of its first printing. Modernism had arrived—again.

Stein's initial obstacle in finding a publisher was not only her revolutionary style, though Hitchcock was not alone in his disregard for the text's ponderous repetition and its impressionistic sense of narrative time. There was also the matter of *Three Lives*'s formal project, which holds its three stories discrete while still vaguely asserting their interdependence—if not their unity. The first and third pieces, "The Good Anna" and "The Gentle Lena," study two German immigrant women who work as domestic servants. The longer and more ambitious piece in the middle, "Melanctha," is a portrait of a biracial woman. The three women live in the same fictional town, Bridgepoint, and loosely share some thematic experiences. All women, two of them immigrants and the other considered an African American, they live on the margins of turn-of-the-century America, and they all experience profound alienation from their families and peers. But their lives do not intersect in any concrete way, certainly not in any common plot. The book's subtitle, "Stories of the Good Anna, Melanctha, and the Gentle Lena," gestures toward this miscellany of form.[3] And yet *Three Lives* still bears a trace of a conventional narrative arc, ending with Lena's marriage and childbearing years, troubled as they are. In this way, notwithstanding its subtitle, Stein's short book stands apart from single-author anthologies, which assert no unity beyond authorship—the posthumous collection *Poe: Poetry, Tales, and Selected Essays*, for example, or *The Portable Faulkner* (1946), which Malcolm Cowley edited with the author's assent. In the dim outlines of a narrative arc, *Three Lives* is more closely related to the short story cycles that would later become a hallmark of American modernism, such as Sherwood Anderson's *Winesburg, Ohio* (1919) and Ernest Hemingway's *In Our Time* (1925). Although many of the first reviews evoked the comfortable label "realism" to describe the text's content, likely owing to the Jamesian depth of its psychological profiles, they found no such familiarity in the text's narrative architecture. One reviewer could do no more than proclaim that "the originality of its narrative form is as notable" as its character studies ("Fiction" 10). Carl Van Vechten, writing the introduction to the Modern Library edition, holds that "every detail represents the whole and is essential to it" but then promptly proceeds to catalogue the three stories independently, thereby undermining the text's ability to integrate its component parts (x). Stein's experiment led others to chase after programmatic labels in an effort to bring order to *Three Lives*'s form, with one reviewer, perhaps in desperation, describing Stein as a "futurist in writing" ("A Futurist Novel" 13). Hitchcock and early readers of Stein, in other words, were challenged to construct and confront a new set of questions to deal with this innovation in form. By what narrative devices are these characters connected? Or do the stories instead pose a complete atomization of the social landscape? Is there any remnant of the coherence of literary realism in this new aesthetics?

In this formal experiment, *Three Lives* inaugurates the central challenge of aesthetic modernism: the dialectical interplay of fragmentation and totality.

Criticism of Stein's short book continues to grapple with matters of style, even as it has broadened its scope to other concerns, particularly race and sexuality.[4] But the thorny problem of *Three Lives*'s form remains underexamined, even though it is instructive for scholars of modernisms. This formal challenge signals the tension of fragment and whole that motivates—or haunts—the full spectrum of modernist work: in turn-of-the-century popular entertainment, the disconnected acts of a vaudeville show that assembled into a whole performance; in poetry, the ruins of T. S. Eliot's *The Waste Land* (1922); in the visual arts, Picasso's and Georges Braque's inventions of collage in 1912 and later the Spanish artist Joan Miró's Constellations series from 1939–41; in music, the fragmentary melodies and halting rhythms of Igor Stravinsky's *The Rite of Spring* (1913). Taking place across continents, manifesting in all forms of art, spanning the divide of the avant-garde and the popular, this modernism was truly global, and its dialectic of fragment and totality was its most durable feature. *Networks of Modernism* studies this open tension, which I call the cultural logic of modernism, and finds a purportedly postmodern figure, the network, to be the figure by which fragment and whole are mediated, and by which American moderns were imagining new models of community.

In other words, it is not so much the meaning but our understanding of the event—*Three Lives* or, more broadly, the onset of modernisms—that lags behind by several decades, illuminated by the advent of the network as the dominant figure of postmodernity. To look at that figure today, I think it is fair to say that the network is nearing—or perhaps has already achieved—the saturation of both contemporary narrative and theoretical production. The former hinges mostly on a profusion of texts that narrativize the six-degrees-of-separation formula. Popularized in a spate of 1990s and 2000s films,[5] such narratives tend to assemble networks of characters along two planes: first, by demonstrating their physical connectedness, signaled by scenes in which characters unknowingly cross paths on the street or conduct some kind of fleeting business or social transaction; and second, by establishing shared themes that loosely tie the characters together, such as existential agony in P. T. Anderson's *Magnolia* (1999) or racial discrimination in Paul Haggis's *Crash* (2005). Such texts have proliferated so quickly that scholars such as David Bordwell have codified their shared conventions under the aegis of a supposedly new genre, "the network narrative." And they have expanded at such a rate that their particular formulation of networks has become a commonplace with a diminishing market: *6°*, J. J. Abrams's primetime television drama that ABC introduced for the 2006–07 season to capitalize on this formula lasted a mere thirteen episodes and was cancelled without so much as a series finale, marking the dénouement of a once-bankable narrative design.

The path is similar in the field of critical theory, where a great proportion of intellectual output over the last thirty or forty years has operated on various networked configurations. I am thinking of the prominence in poststructuralist thought of distributive figures such as Michel Foucault's panopticon, Gilles Deleuze and Félix Guatarri's rhizome, and Donna Haraway's cyborg; of the rhizome's reformulation in Michael Hardt and Antonio Negri's *Empire* trilogy (2000–09); of Bruno Latour's advocacy of actor-network theory; and of Manuel Castells's *The Rise of the Network Society* (1996), which declares that informational capitalism operates on an "organizational logic" that itself renders the logic of the network "more powerful than the powers in the network" (208); of singularity as it is studied by thinkers such as Giorgio Agamben; of theorists of digital media and hypertextuality, such as Michael Joyce, George P. Landow, and Stuart Moulthrop; of the rise of network analysis methodologies throughout the digital humanities. Hardt and Negri stand out in this list because they assert the political necessity of networks in an age of globalization, writing in the preface to *Multitude* (2004) that the multitude, which is a "network that provides the means of encounter so that we can work and live in common," itself embodies "the possibility of democracy on a global scale" (xii–xiv, xi). But again the expansion of the network seems to approach a limit, particularly in the reevaluation of the network's political potential. Even Hardt and Negri concede that the network is ambivalent, as it is also the organizing principle of the imperial. "Network power," they call it. Likewise, Alexander R. Galloway and Eugene Thacker claim in *The Exploit* (2007) that the model has no inherent politics at all, writing of network organization in the United States military and Al Qaeda alike: "It will not do simply to assign a political content to a network form. Worse would be to claim that a network form is innately reactionary or progressive" (13). "We're tired of rhizomes," they conclude, before calling for new models of resistance and new means of relating the human to the nonhuman (153).

Observing this trajectory of the network through contemporary narrative and theoretical work, I am also struck by the inability of a heterogeneous field of theoretical projects to shake up the very narrow formulation of networks espoused by six-degrees narratives. The correspondence of the two discourses is, in fact, a historical contingency. If we turn our attention from the postmodern to the modern, we will see that the network has a longer history and a much wider understanding than it has taken after the dawn of the digital age. Indeed, even Galloway and Thacker, ever skeptical about the revolutionary potential of the network, grant that it "may have been accurate in previous decades" of the twentieth century to assert the liberatory promise of distributed organization (13). Such a moment, I argue, is modernism: in the ferment of social upheaval and aesthetic experiment, the moderns found the network a versatile model for their radical reformulations of social space, which often anticipate the figure as it is celebrated by Hardt and Negri.

Stein's *Three Lives* is an instructive early case study in this phenomenon and plots a new graphing of the intellectual history Galloway and Thacker allow for. The text creates meaning in the interstices of its three character studies and challenges the reader to assemble the three stories by identifying and reflecting on their points of connection as well as the deep spatial and temporal gaps that divide them. In form, the stories distribute their characters by prohibiting them from even a cursory interaction—the type of fleeting cameo one might expect from a six-degrees narrative—and those gaps are often reinforced in the stories' content. For instance, Melanctha, the biracial young woman whose plot involves her "wanderings" into promiscuity, is upbraided when her adventures take her into the white world of Bridgepoint. Her friend Rose scolds her, "no I never do say to you Melanctha, you hadn't never ought to be with white men, though it ain't never the way I feel it ever real right for a decent colored girl to be always doing, but not never Melanctha now you hear me, no not never no kind of white men like you been with always now Melanctha when I see you" (123–24). The work of assembling *Three Lives* into a totalizing narrative requires readers to think broadly about each story's role in the outline of the book. For example, one might read the three stories as creating a disjointed pastiche of the romance: Anna's story details a mundane working life, Melanctha's covers a sexual awakening, and Lena's brings narrative closure with a marriage and children. *Three Lives* resists any happy returns in each of its component parts, however. Anna's domestic work ultimately grinds her to death; Melanctha finds no fulfillment but only new experiences of suffering in each relationship; and Lena is mired in a loveless arranged marriage before dying as she delivers her fourth child, a stillborn.

Read this way, the formal project of *Three Lives* provides yet another register of Stein's revolution against earlier regimes of aesthetics. Still more broadly, in this reading there emerges a new understanding of social space in which the margins become more visible and traditional centers of power are scrutinized, even distributed.

Our vocabulary for networks today is rooted in the languages of informational technologies and graph theory. Points are referred to as "nodes" or "vertices," and the lines that connect them are called "edges." The volume of nodes constitutes the "order" of a network, with the number of edges determining its "size." A node's "degree" measures the number of edges that connect to it: a "hub" node measures high in degree, whereas a "leaf" node is an outlier with only one edge connecting to it. This language also allows us to see networks in different shapes. Centralized networks originate from one source and allow the dissemination of information to a multitude of destinations. Decentralized networks operate from several points of origin. And distributed networks facilitate exchanges from a multitude of origins. Galloway and Thacker describe the first form as "pyramidal, hierarchical schemes," the second as "a core 'backbone' of hubs each with radiating peripheries," and the third as "a collection of node-to-node relations with no backbone and no center" (32). Though Stein and the other moderns studied in *Networks of Modernism* lacked this vocabulary, the distributed form plays a crucial role in their mediation of fragment and totality. In fact, I think Van Vechten's introduction to the Modern Library edition of *Three Lives* is casting about for such a vocabulary when he notes the influence of Paul Cézanne. In Van Vechten's reading, Cézanne displaces any genealogy of literary realism for Stein's book, despite the appearances of Jamesian psychological studies in its character portraits. Van Vechten writes, "the planes and distorted lines of that great painter are definitely to be discovered in Miss Stein's sturdy prose" (ix). Planes and lines, nodes and edges—these are the fundamental units of a distributed aesthetics that intervenes into the binaries of fragment and whole.

This cultural logic of modernism obtains not only in aesthetic experiments like Stein's. It is also expressed in the tension between homogeneity and dispersal, the polarity that defined a host of the period's social, economic, and technological developments. In modern America, this tension has a shifting politics. Homogeneity was sometimes embraced as a coherent Americanism and at other times held suspect as a massifying erosion of the individual.

Dispersal for some meant the disarray of the nation and for others preserved the individual from the degradations of mass culture. In modernist aesthetics, this dialectic manifests as a tension between totality and fragment, the two most basic tendencies of high modernism that are on display in *Three Lives*. This cultural logic holds in global modernisms, but especially in American modernism, in which experiments in the paradoxes of totalization and fragmentation performed important work to rethink the meaning of national space and national belonging in response to seismic shifts in the nation's demographic makeup and to refigurations of the center and the periphery wrought by technological innovations and by ever-evolving systems of global trade. Many of the moderns looked to the distributed network to mediate this dialectical tension, negotiating the competing visions of dispersal and unity into a system that accommodates both through its nodal, interconnective configuration. For these reasons, *Networks of Modernism* positions the network as the defining figure of American modernism and explores its use as a conceptual tool that American moderns relied on to grapple with the changing American landscape. This study not only reinvigorates the network during its downward turn in contemporary narrative and theory. An emphasis on networks in modernist thought and aesthetics will also align our understanding of the projects of modernism more closely with the way the moderns were trying to think their own milieu.

Networks of the Modern Period

To situate the network at the core of modernist production, I should first acknowledge that a conventional history of network discourses tends to operate within a fairly short timeline. The *Oxford English Dictionary* dates the first uses of the term "network" to the sixteenth century, when it describes textiles and metal fabrication, but it is as if the ideational and organizational power of the term originated autochthonously somewhere around the third quarter of the twentieth century. It is not just that our vocabulary for networks is informed by technologies of the digital age or that the network has presided over narrative and theoretical work at the turn of the twenty-first century. The network is also taken axiomatically to be the signal metaphor for this period, whether describing advances of the digital revolution, the flows of capital and information in the age of globalization, or the breaks of poststructuralism from the binaries and hierarchies of structuralism—in sum, the very lived experience of postmodernity. This truncated history of networks, as well as their confinement in narrative to the six-degrees theory, signals a high degree of amnesia for—or perhaps a misreading of—much of the work and social experience from earlier in the twentieth century that provide another and perhaps a richer archive of network discourses.

Lacking our informational vocabulary, the moderns understood the network intuitively in its distributed sense. The absence of a proper modernist manifesto celebrating an aesthetics of networks may obscure the use of this important figuration for some readers; the following chapter, on Randolph Bourne's 1916 essay "Trans-National America," addresses this problem. Nevertheless, the imperative to imagine distributed social space was written across the modern landscape. The changing social, economic, demographic, and technological conditions at the beginning of the twentieth century called for new models of thinking about national and global communities. For example, Guglielmo Marconi's famed transatlantic radio transmission in 1901 signaled the onset of global wireless communications, requiring new ways to think about the local, the global, and their interrelationship. Likewise, in completing the first transcontinental telephone line in 1915, the American Telegraph and Telephone Company boldly promised to make "a neighborhood of a nation."[6] The steady advance of urbanization forced people, especially in the United States, to reconceive the boundaries and shapes of community, the interrelationships of center and periphery, and the meanings of pluralism and regionalism. The expansion of American cities, paired with advances in electric lighting and public transportation, facilitated a public culture that led people to reexamine social interrelationships in the new "era of the crowd." The increased mobility of the period brought more than twenty million European immigrants—many of whom were non-Protestants and considered people of color—to the United States, demanding reconceptualization of the nation's identity. The destabilization of global trade that followed World War I reconfigured trading partnerships and accordingly prompted new understandings of markets and neighbors, commodities and strangers.

The radio offers a case study of the modernist dialectic of centralization and dispersal. At the turn of the century, the airwaves were a mess of conflicting signals. Radio enthusiasts were free to choose their own frequencies, could transmit as far as their wattage allowed, and were not restricted to any regular scheduling that listeners could reliably tune in to. The result was an outright cacophony of overlapping signals. The airwaves were so chaotic that transmissions detailing such important news as the sinking of the *Titanic* and the ensuing rescue efforts were routinely interrupted by competing signals. This situation provides two illustrations of the dialectic of unity and dispersal. On the one hand, it was becoming clear that radio technology itself, which had at first been intended for point-to-point communications between two parties on the model of the electrical telegraph or telephone, simply was not complying with the objective of perfectly linear transmissions. This was demonstrated during the interference of *Titanic* transmissions and later with transmissions during World War I, which military leaders could not trust to be received confidentially by a single targeted audience in the field. By the 1920s, broadcasting, the multivalent scattering of signals across the airwaves to a widely dispersed audience, was understood to be radio's fundamental purpose, displacing presumptions about its role as a device of linear, centrally controlled communications. On the other hand, the untenable chaos of the airwaves called for a series of regulatory reforms, begun by the Radio Act of 1912, which began to articulate the airwaves as the domain of federal government instead of individual radio enthusiasts. In *Hello, Everybody* (2008), Anthony Rudel explains the tension that arose as Herbert Hoover, then secretary of commerce, led efforts to license stations and assign them to specific frequencies. Put simply, hobbyists who used the airwaves to talk with each other and listen to news from distant places came into conflict with powerful companies that saw commercial interests in radio technology and broadcasting (50). As with the technology of its transmissions, the social space of the radio also staged this dialectical tension, as governmental and corporate interests aimed to make the chaotic airwaves safe for commerce, while individual radio enthusiasts wanted to preserve the public element of free radio transmissions.

By November of 1928, with the help of the Radio Act of 1927, the regulatory campaign finally achieved the reallocations of frequencies and wattage limits, rendering the nation a fixed system of radio broadcasting. Through the 1920s, the explosive growth of radio programming and the widening of broadcast ranges were reflected in the wild expansion of the listening audience: in 1922, there were an estimated 60,000 radio sets in American homes, and by 1929 that number had ballooned to around 7.5 million (Rudel 105). The full coverage of the nation's radio waves, paired with the aggressive expansion of ownership of radio sets that would continue into the Depression years, made radio broadcasts a key feature of the national space. With the aid of relay networks established by corporate interests, people could hear broadcasts from across the nation, detailing news of national and regional importance. WGN, for example, had broadcast the Scopes Trial in 1925—the first live coverage of its kind—with the *Chicago Tribune* trumpeting the broadcasts as "a demonstration of the public service of radio in communicating to the masses great news events" (Larson 142). Throughout the 1920s, broadcasts of election results became a national pastime, with restaurants and even prisons organizing events around the radio coverage (Rudel 120–21). Such coverage mixed national returns and local returns so that listeners became familiar with not only their own local results but also the local results being broadcast from distant stations. The network of lines and radio signals that made such broadcasts possible in turn created a network of listeners who were beginning to think of their national space as a network, in turn. The limitations of a given radio set might determine how we define such organization in today's informational language: a collection of radios designed only to receive signals would compose part of a decentralized network, whereas radios capable of both sending and receiving signals would compose a fully distributed body. But these distinctions would be anachronistic to the moderns, for whom the advent of the radio prompted a general distributed understanding of the United States.

The American corporation provides another register of emerging network models during the period, introducing a vast public to this form of organization through the lived experience of the rapidly changing workplace. The modern corporation is often held to be strictly hierarchical, monolithic, and centralized. But when contextualized between the dominant organizations that preceded and followed it, the modern corporation's movement toward distributed models appears in relief. Alan Trachtenberg's essential work *The Incorporation of America* (1982) posits that the Gilded Age corporation remade American culture in its own image as a "more tightly structured society with new hierarchies of control" (3–4). In contrast, sociologist Manuel Castells demonstrates how contemporary corporations embrace the networked formations of the postmodern, global era: today's multinational corporation is composed of "semi-autonomous units" organized around different markets and products.[7] What happens between these periods is not the continuation of Gilded Age hierarchy until the multinational arrives to deliver a decisive break. Rather, the modern period marks the emergence of networks in the evolution of corporate organization.

The Modern Corporation and Private Property (1932), the foundational study of corporate governance by Adolf Berle and Gardiner Means, measures some of the stakes of these nascent developments in corporate organization. The book's central argument is that corporations were enervating the traditional institution of private property with a system of "multiple ownership." Berle and Means contend that the corporation's signal intervention is the separation of owning stockholders from the managerial control of the corporations.[8] This phenomenon creates a paradox, as the increased dispersal of stock ownership results in the increased centralization of power by corporate managers. This consolidation of power—by managers and by corporate firms generally—was a major concern during the modern period. Matthew Josephson's *The Robber Barons* (1934), for example, studies the consolidation of wealth through the paths of captains of industry such as Andrew Carnegie, Pierpont Morgan, John D. Rockefeller, Cornelius Vanderbilt, and others whose corporate firms heavily influenced the American economy and nearly constituted an oligarchy. Josephson laments the centralization of corporate power, writing that when these men entered history, "the United States was a mercantile-agrarian democracy. When they departed or retired from active life, it was something else: a unified industrial society, the effective economic control of which was lodged in the hands of a hierarchy" (vii). Fears of the modern corporation's centralizing powers would result in the Clayton Act of 1914, a piece of antitrust legislation that prohibited dealings between firms that could lessen market competition.

But in addition to responding to the threat of a monolithic hierarchy, the Clayton Act also demonstrates the emergence of network organization in the modern corporation. As Mark Mizruchi puts it in *The American Corporate Network, 1904–1974* (1982), the primary goal of the legislation was to outlaw "interlocks between competing companies within particular industries" (99). In other words, while the centralizing power of a single corporation was worrisome, the potential for multiple firms to interconnect and expand their sphere of influence demanded regulation. Mizruchi ultimately finds that the Clayton Act had little impact on intercorporation networking, but its very passage demonstrates awareness that it was not only the centralizing force of the corporation but also the power of networked corporations that would require regulatory attention.[9]

In response to atomizing legislation such as the Clayton Act and the ever-present imperative to grow, the modern corporation began a process of internal diversification—the expansion of operations to house new, often unrelated projects within the same firm, acting as the inverse of outsourcing—to sidestep the limits placed on interlocking relationships. Jon Didrichsen locates this development in the 1920s, which saw the onset of "the large, diversified, multidivisional firm in the United States" (38).[10] In Didrichsen's account, a firm that diversified to expand its profits would meet challenges with the myriad technologies, manufacturing demands, distribution channels, and managerial exigencies of the new line, and this resulted in the decentralized, multidivisional model of organization that typifies the multinational (39). This organizational process, he writes, "was pioneered by Du Pont and General Motors in the 1920's and was soon accepted by firms in the chemical, motor vehicle, and electrical industries" (39). The rippling effects later spread to "processors of agricultural products and the oil and rubber industries," but the fully networked conglomerate did not arrive until the early 1950s (39–40). Under the façade of its controlled hierarchy, the modern corporation was experimenting with distributed organization—"multidivisional" if not yet fully multinational.

Again, radio provides a case study for this organizational model. The Radio Corporation of America (RCA) was formed in 1919 by the General Electric Company (GE) at the behest of the Navy Department, which was concerned about the British-owned Marconi Company of America's administration of United States airwaves (Rudel 23). GE, presumably, was the logical choice for this acquisition because of its deep pockets and its expertise in electronics. The link between radio production and radio broadcasting is of course only nominal, but throughout the 1920s it provided a model followed by many other firms—Westinghouse Electric Company, Crosley Manufacturing Company, Love Electric, and others—that established or bought up radio stations across the country with the goal of building demand for the products they were already manufacturing (31, 63–67). When these companies' dominion of the airwaves was seen to verge on restraint of trade, the National Broadcasting Company (NBC) was created in 1926, owned 50 percent by RCA, 30 percent by GE, and 20 percent by Westinghouse (93). Now separated into autonomous firms, GE and RCA took on responsibilities in addition to their original missions of manufacturing and broadcasting to include the unfamiliar work of entertainment programming.[11] GE and RCA, through the mediating link of NBC, demonstrate two models of networked corporate organization in the modern period: on the one hand, they are formally separate firms involved in internal diversification, but on the other hand, their mutual entanglement places them in an external network of corporate interests.

Whereas GE, RCA, and NBC cluster together in electronics manufacturing, radio broadcast, and entertainment programming, Du Pont embraced a more expansive form of internal diversification through the 1920s. Du Pont's first objective was to produce organic chemicals and related products in synthetic fibers, and in the process of advancing these products the corporation's research led it to new terrain in such disparate fields as photographic film, pharmaceuticals, advanced instruments, and precious metal compositions (Didrichsen 41). The corporation's organizational structure diversified to match its miscellaneous interests, creating a networked array under Du Pont's homogenizing title (42). This diversification—of production but also of institutional organization—is cast against the high degree of financial and operating controls Du Pont exercised over its production departments, demonstrating the centralized accumulation of power that so concerned Berle and Means and Josephson (42).

The complex array of corporate interrelations—among GE, RCA, and NBC, for instance, or within Du Pont—was increasingly common throughout the modern period as the corporation evolved from the static hierarchies of the Gilded Age. These developments put on display the period's dialectical tension of unity and dispersal. I emphasize corporate organization because it is not restricted to business. Just as Trachtenberg argues that the hierarchical Gilded Age corporation effected "a more general process of change, the reorganization of perceptions as well as of enterprise and institutions," so does modern diversification prompt a "reorganization of perceptions" (3). This "remaking of cultural perceptions," as Trachtenberg says of the former era, informed all manner of modern life, ranging from the decentralization of family life to an emergent aesthetics of networks. However, whereas Trachtenberg argues that the Gilded Age corporation initializes these changes across American culture, I argue that in the modern period the logic of network organization emerges from several centers—the corporation being a particularly powerful one.

Complementing the networked social reorganization undertaken by radio technology and corporate diversification are the ideational, ideological, and epistemological revolutions that typified the modern milieu. Albert Einstein's theory of relativity, for example, required that the relationship of space and time must be understood as not linear but spatially distributed and interpenetrating processes. The nascent field of anthropology, once an arm of colonial expansion, strove to assuage anxieties about Western culture and overturn theories of scientific racism by emphasizing a cosmopolitan appreciation for global cultural diversity, challenging provincial values of nation and identity. The advent of labor management and discipline pioneered by Frederick Winslow Taylor and Henry Ford redistributed the linear, sequential flow of production in a traditional factory into a coordinated division of labor, reinventing the organization of the workplace and broader paradigms of social organization. The public intellectual Randolph Bourne, whose essay "Trans-National America" is the subject of the following chapter, asserted a distributed vision of national space and ethnic identity to mediate the competing discourses of homogeneous Americanism and diasporic pluralism during the preparedness debates that set the course for the United States' entry into the Great War. These fields of intellectual production stage the beginnings of a revolt against the conventionally linear and hierarchical chains of space, people, and work. With the credibility of those old models in crisis, network organization emerges to order modern knowledge.

Of course, these interventions did not go unchallenged. Although the radio and the corporation were two sites introducing distributed social space, the emergence of mass culture, ushered in in no small part by the radio, was establishing a monolithic understanding of the nation. Celebrated by some, this massification was often treated with derisive representations of crowds in modern narrative or with scorn by modern aesthetes—for example, in F. R. Leavis's *Mass Civilization and Minority Culture* (1930) or Clement Greenberg's "Avant-Garde and Kitsch" (1939). Not only some moderns' concern over the future—or even their present—state of aesthetics was at stake; the very nature of social space also hung in the balance in polemics against massification. Dwight Macdonald's late modern reassertion of high aesthetics, "Masscult and Midcult" (1960), identifies this underlying issue, arguing that "the masses are in historical time what a crowd is in space: a large quantity of people unable to express their human qualities because they are related to each other neither as individuals nor as members of a community. In fact, they are not related *to each other* at all but only to some impersonal, abstract, crystallizing factor" (8).

In other words, a massified nation and its local analogue, the crowd, threaten the erosion of traditional social space—particularly the knowable community. The friction between these competing models for imagining national space reveals the heart of the matter: community, at its widest and its narrowest meanings, would require a new shape to adapt to the exigencies of the period.

Just as the network does not emerge autochthonously with postmodernity, neither can the modern period claim it outright. The nineteenth century was already beginning to register this new organization in the emergence of the railroads and the electrical telegraph. Rail tracks proliferated wildly over the middle part of the century.[12] By around 1840 the rail system had covered some 3,000 miles of tracks after a decade of slow growth. The completion of the transcontinental line in 1869 established more and more rail lines extending across the West, so that by 1890 there were 90,000 miles of track crisscrossing the country. The rail system peaked in 1916 with a total of 254,000 miles, but by that point the distribution of the American landscape was already a *fait accompli*: before the new century, the railways had transcended state boundaries and reformulated the axial relationships of the urban and the rural, the East and the West, the North and the South—and in their maps made visible the distribution of national space. A residuum of this older register of networks appears in the content of Stein's *Three Lives*, reinforcing the text's distributed form. Melanctha finds the rail yards "a ceaseless fascination" because they give her a modest connection to the West and the South and provide the excitement of "a free and whirling future" (55). Performing a similar role in communications, the electrical telegraph had become a commonplace in the United States by the Civil War.[13] The technology was qualitatively different from that of Marconi's transatlantic transmission and the advances in radio that followed, but the social space fashioned by wired and wireless communications was different only by a matter of degree. The railroad and the electrical telegraph are tied together not only in the indexes of nineteenth-century history but often shared the same physical space, as telegraph lines were routinely constructed in the right-of-way alongside rail tracks. And this history reaches back still further, as Richard R. John writes in *Network Nation* (2010), reminding us that the electrical telegraph took its name from the optical telegraph that was developed in France in the 1790s.[14]

The modern period, then, is best understood as an intensification in this long history of network organization, not as a point of origin. The clearest marker of difference between this period and those that preceded it is an abrupt break in aesthetics, such as the one posed by the formal project of Stein's *Three Lives*. Indeed, although the railroads and the electrical telegraph mark the beginnings of a reorganized social space, the aesthetics that correspond to those developments is little interested in such a reorganization project. Rather, the realist works that typify the later stages of the nineteenth century and appear residually in the first decades of the twentieth strive for a coherent unity—one that allows for complexity, to be sure, but one that cannot abide the fragmentation that would become a hallmark of modernist aesthetics. Modern technology, work, and thought index the myriad centers from which network discourses were proliferating at the outset of the twentieth century. Their common investment in the dialectical tension of centralization and dispersal, unity and fragment, demonstrates the entanglement of social experience and intellectual production that comprises the cultural logic of modernism. However, the center that retains a special privilege in this intellectual history—and the one that is the focus of *Networks of Modernism*—is modernist aesthetics, which is produced by these discourses while simultaneously intervening in them with adoptions and manipulations of network models that offered the moderns outlets for grappling with the crises of their milieu.

Networks of Modern Aesthetics

The moderns' investments in networked configurations manifest in a variety of the period's trademark experiments in the arts, such as collage in the visual arts and montage in film, and especially in the narrative experiments that are the subject of the following chapters. American modernists responded to the dramatic changes of their milieu, both recognizing the advent of the network as a social discourse and adopting it to rethink the nature of their art and its relation to life in the United States and abroad. Whether committed to popular modernisms or the experiments of the avant-garde, they found the network a helpful figure for negotiating the social dialectic of centralization and dispersal and its aesthetic corollary, that of fragment and totality.

Before addressing modernist narrative, I want to contextualize its experiments with networks amid the broader experiments of modernist aesthetics, especially collage and its kin, montage. These two visual arts are in close dialogue with the subjects of later chapters on Jean Toomer's *Cane* (1923) and

John Dos Passos's *U.S.A.* trilogy (1930–36), demonstrating the interplay of modern experiments in distributed form. Collage is an umbrella term for several techniques—papier collé, assemblage, decoupage, photomontage, montage, and so on—that share a common logic of dismemberment, simultaneity, and integration, and in the process challenge traditional assumptions about surface. As Marjorie Perloff writes, collage challenges "the representability of the sign" (10). The technique was pioneered with Picasso's *Still Life with Chair Caning* and Braque's *Fruit Dish*—both debuted in 1912, though art historians, to say nothing of the dispute between the artists themselves, disagree about whose piece came first—and became a staple of global modernisms. But collage nonetheless acquired a distinctly American character because of its association with advertisement and commodification.

The logic of collage lies in the visualization of networked space. Often collage is discussed as operating on a simple, static logic of juxtaposition, when instead a work of collage creates myriad links of meaning on a more fully integrated, distributed model. Such works rely on a spatialized semiotics, creating conspicuous lacunae between some images and striking juxtapositions between others to foster proliferating relationships of incongruities across the field of vision. Jean-Jacques Thomas relates this to a hermeneutic of networks, writing that collage subverts any kind of "graphic accumulation" and instead establishes "new networks of significance" (80). In other words, the creation of meaning takes place in the interstices of different images and materials, and this representational strategy can be read as an inherently networked formulation: the viewer must assemble the disparate images into one whole or another by imagining the relational lines of connection and disconnection that generate the piece's meaning.

Montage operates on a similar scheme, involving not only spatial but also temporal breaks and linkages that the viewer assembles into an integrated, if not altogether coherent, unit. Montage is, of course, a formal relative of collage, and like collage it is an umbrella term that groups together a set of techniques in film—sequential revolutions, overlays, split images, mirrored images, and so on—that deconstruct narrative linearity and challenge even the possibility of realist representation. Associated with the pioneering work of D. W. Griffith in the 1910s and the still more experimental work of Sergei Eisenstein and Dziga Vertov in the 1920s, montage is often assumed to be an intrinsically Russian form, though of course it quickly became a common technique of popular and experimental film—although in varying degrees of intensity. Like collage, montage is often described in terms of juxtaposition, creating its meaning out of the collision of conflicting images. But again I think this understanding oversimplifies the form's insistence on an integrated whole, privileging local disjunctures over the constellar assembly of the entire piece. Walter Benjamin underscores montage's totalizing impulse in *The Arcades Project* (1982), itself an exercise in what he describes as "literary montage," writing that the technique asks the viewer to "assemble large-scale constructions out of the smallest and most precisely cut components. Indeed, to discover in the analysis of the small individual moment the crystal of the total event" (461). The dialectical nature of the process Benjamin describes is best understood as a networked strategy of representation and interpretation: artist and viewer alike construct a web of meanings from the host of potential connections among the disparate images and sounds into a convergent whole.

The common project of collage and montage—indeed, the defining feature across high modernist aesthetics—lies in the paradox of formal fragmentation and totalization. This is true also of modern American narrative, in which even the standard literary encyclopedia situates the fragment as a stock trope and totality as its always-already partner in interwar fiction. These competing impulses—to represent a society breaking into pieces under the pressures of rapid social change, and simultaneously to find a semblance of unity to guard against outright entropy—coincide in the form, as well as the content, of major works of high modernism. To leave these tensions as a sort of unresolved critical ambiguity, however, performs a major disservice to signal innovations of the modern period—namely, the mediation of the fragment/totality binary through the network. As the spatial and temporal interconnections of collage and montage demonstrate, this binary is untenable and instead should be considered as posing two extremes in a constellar system.

American modernists used network figuration to rethink the very meaning of wholeness and to generate new models for understanding the changing dynamics of national space. In this respect, the fragment/totality binary presents a false choice to readers of modern works: either an entropic state of fragmentation or a smooth totality predicated on nostalgia for the mythic wholeness of a bygone past. Rather, a distributed aesthetics allowed the moderns to envision a national space that would withstand the crises of the period precisely because it posed a new model of community. Not only did the moderns use this conceptual tool to rethink the boundaries of representation as part of the modernist rejection of realist conventions, but they also discovered its usefulness in rethinking the milieu of the modern period. They found in networked models a set of opportunities to articulate major societal changes and to expand the conventions of representation corresponding to the changing American landscape. The network, as later chapters will show, proved handy in renovating national identity after the failure of the melting pot, in rethinking the changing configurations of race in America, in reimagining the interrelated nature of the class system, in redrawing the contours of history and historical study, and in reenvisioning the core dynamics of democracy—issues that demanded reconsideration in light of the modern period's raft of transformations.

The short story cycle presents one example of this radical work in the formal composition of modernist narrative. The typical conventions of this genre involve a set of stories linked—by plot, character, setting, thematic patterns, and so on—so tightly that the composite rendering of the individual texts deepens the component parts and the whole text alike. The proliferation of the short story cycle across modern American writing signals its stature as one of the period's trademark innovations: Willa Cather's *The Troll Garden* (1905), the collective novel *The Whole Family* (1908), Stein's *Three Lives*, Henry James's *The Finer Grain* (1910), Edith Wharton's *Tales of Men and Ghosts* (1910), Sherwood Anderson's *Winesburg, Ohio*, Waldo Frank's *City Block* (1922), Ernest Hemingway's *In Our Time*, Thornton Wilder's *The Bridge of San Luis Rey* (1927), John Steinbeck's *Tortilla Flat* (1935), Zora Neale Hurston's *Mules and Men* (1935), Richard Wright's *Uncle Tom's Children* (1938), and William Faulkner's *The Unvanquished* (1938)—to give but a survey of the many texts scholars point to when establishing the short story cycle's emergence in American modernism.

A typical treatment of a short story cycle places the text as vacillating between fragment and totality. On the one hand, a short story cycle may appear to be a volume or portfolio of the writer's "greatest hits," collecting disparate short fiction and in some cases poems as well. On the other hand, the text also carries a totalizing impulse that transcends its diverse texts: the author's avoidance of titles suggesting assortment or merely replicating the title of a shorter work provides an early cue that the work aspires to some kind of integration of the component texts. Both of these regimes are insufficient, however, because they do not account for the short story cycle's networked logic of interplay—as in, for instance, the readings earlier in this chapter of *Three Lives*'s form as a pastiche of the romance and the text's distributed investment in the social margins.

A survey of the scholarship on this genre shows an implicit recognition of this interplay, though the term "network" never rises to the level of direct scrutiny. Forrest L. Ingram's *Representative Short Story Cycles of the Twentieth Century* (1971), Susan Garland Mann's *The Short Story Cycle* (1989), Maggie Dunn and Ann Morris's *The Composite Novel* (1995)—each of these studies casts the short story cycle as a nodal construction of autonomous units whose complete meaning can only be understood in relation to an array of other texts. Like collage, this spatialized semiotics takes place not only between neighboring texts but is distributed across the entire aggregate. Ingram, for example, describes the genre as "a set of stories linked to each other in such a way as to maintain a balance between the individuality of each of the stories and the necessities of the large unit" (15). Mann writes that in the genre "the stories are both self-sufficient and interrelated" (15). Dunn and Morris describe the text's organization as "a tissue of fine connectives" (13). These studies may ultimately emphasize a smooth coherence of totality rather than the paradoxes and tensions of constellar space, but nonetheless their language gestures toward the distinctly modern experience of networks presented in this distinctly modern genre.

Acting as a network spanning its constitutive texts, the short story cycle works in a variety of ways to rethink national space. Texts such as *Three Lives*, Anderson's *Winesburg, Ohio*, or Steinbeck's *Tortilla Flat* operate on an axis of place that bridges center and periphery to create connective lines that readers could replicate in other contexts. Other texts, such as Wilder's *The Bridge of San Luis Rey*, articulate modernist problems of temporality with networks that link together generations of development into a coherent system. In other words, by bridging chasms of time and place with multidimensional linking mechanisms, the short story cycle negotiates the moderns' cultural logic of centralization and dispersal, mediating this dialectical tension with distributed systems.

Why does the modern period lay claim to the proliferation of the short story cycle? The short story had been established for some half century or longer, so why do we not see it prevail in, for example, the American Renaissance? Mann finds a correspondence between the rise of the short story cycle and the profusion of avant-garde "little magazines," such as the *Dial* and the *Masses*, that, along with such major-market publications as the *Saturday Evening Post*, made the short story a bankable project for many modernist writers.[15] But the profusion of little magazines is insufficient to explain this modern phenomenon, given the boom in printing capabilities that made story writing a professional endeavor for Poe, Hawthorne, and their contemporaries. There is still room to read more complexity in the relationship between this emergent genre and the milieu from which it arose.

Not merely the byproduct of trends in magazine publication, the short story cycle is a mode of formal experimentation that modernists could use to render the ruptures and ligatures that were changing the features and meaning of American culture. In *Winesburg, Ohio*, for example, Anderson explores the stories of several different figures connected by setting, by their relation to the bildungsroman character George Willard, and by thematic likenesses such as loneliness, restlessness, and the grotesque. Anderson's perspectivist rendering of a rural Victorian-era town deconstructs mythic understandings of unity, rendering Winesburg not a monolithically unified social formation but a network of its constituents. Hemingway's *In Our Time*, by contrast, offers no unity of plot, setting, or character: some of its stories feature the maturation of Nick Adams, other stories have nothing whatsoever to do with this protagonist, and the vignettelike interchapters are still further removed from Nick's development. *In Our Time* is a much more disparate set of texts than those oriented around the township of Winesburg. But scholars such as Debra Moddelmog have argued that *In Our Time* should be understood as a loosely coordinated narrative by looking at the plot similarities throughout the stories, finding one in which we know Nick to be involved, and deducing that the others have been written by Nick under the mask of an alter ego through a sort of meta-authorship.[16] The result is that *In Our Time* poses a networked self that is assembled across several disparate texts—not a static, monolithic identity but a subjectivity built on a constellar model. In both cases, at the risk of belaboring the issue, Anderson and Hemingway rely on distributed figuration to represent community and subject—strategies of narration that are only thinkable in the context of the network's emergence throughout the modern period.

The prevalence of major-market magazines in the construction of the modernist short story cycle prompts a reconsideration of popular modernisms as well as the formal experimentation of more avant-garde work. Indeed, both popular and avant-garde writers published in magazines like the *Saturday Evening Post* and *Harper's Bazar*, challenging the traditional dichotomy of high and popular modernisms.[17] In the popular works of the period, the use of networks shifts from form to content—often to representation of the public culture that thrived during the modern period and that was itself constitutive of popular modernisms. Susan Hegeman has argued that the modern period was characterized by "a different arrangement of social space than the one we now experience" ("Haunted" 300).[18] This social space put a high value on public gathering. The moderns' public culture, as David Nasaw points out, was facilitated by the shortened workday's creation of leisure time, the electrification projects that turned cities into playgrounds of nightlife entertainments, and the expansion of public transit—all of which resulted from the sheer human density created by urbanization (3–9). The result of these developments was a spirit of public exchange, as people mixed with unprecedented disregard for traditional social barriers such as ethnicity, religious affiliation, or occupation; the color line still prevailed, however, leaving persons of color to construct separate sites of public culture. This "different arrangement of social space," whose rise and fall generally correspond to the bookends of the modern period, prompted moderns to rethink social formations, often in terms of distributed models.

This public culture manifests in the content of modernist narrative in two ways that draw heavily on networked figuration: representation of public spaces and crowds. The heterogeneity that typifies the space of such public exchanges made for a popular choice of setting in many works. Raucous movie theaters of the nickelodeon era, cavernous movie palaces, the curious sociological site of dance halls, amusement parks attracting people from all walks of life, and city streets themselves—these all provided settings in which strangers mixed freely, defying many of the atomizing norms of class and ethnicity, as well as sex and gender. Writing of 1930s Hollywood film, Rem Koolhaas argues that the hotel, another of these public spaces, served as both a setting and a plot (149–50).

Koolhaas is thinking of films such as Edmund Goulding's *Grand Hotel* (1932), but the same could be said of several other modernist works. For example, Horace McCoy's *They Shoot Horses, Don't They?* (1935) takes place at a dance marathon, one of the unheralded entertainments of the Depression era. The public space of the dance floor facilitates a mix of aspiring stars looking for their big break, the down-and-out looking for a reliable source of food, and criminals on the run looking for a place to blend into the crowd. The dance marathon's system of interchangeable partners constantly invents new links among the dancers, and the patronage of dedicated fans forges links between dancers and their audience, together building an interpersonal network out of the public spaces of the dance marathon. It is no coincidence that modern narratives so often focus on public spaces. For the public space is not merely an inert setting but an agential force of distribution; it forces disparate individuals into contact, and although that contact often falls short of intimate and lifelong ties, it fosters myriad transitory links connecting each individual to the others through innumerable other mediating links—in effect using space itself to create a social network in defiance of stratifying social systems of class, gender, ethnicity, and so on.

In a related fashion, another manifestation of public culture in modernist narrative, the representation of crowds, focuses not on the spatial organization involved in public culture but on the very specific social formation it produced. The modern period was, as Gustave Le Bon famously proclaimed in *The Crowd* (1895), "the era of crowds." Le Bon's writing posed two critical fallacies of social organization that scholars contend with even today. "The substitution of the unconscious action of crowds for the conscious activity of individuals," he wrote, "is one of the principal characteristics of the present age" (3). The crowd demonstrated a mob mentality, one that for Le Bon was associated with the racial makeup of the crowd, drawn from its urban origins. Alongside that first premise, smacking of the period's scientific racism, Le Bon positioned the crowd as innately barbaric and violent. A man who gives himself over to a crowd, according to Le Bon, "possesses the spontaneity of violence, the ferocity, and also the enthusiasm and heroism of primitive beings, whom he further tends to resemble by the facility with which he allows himself to be impressed by words and image" (32). And as the concluding phrase indicates, Le Bon projected both of these characteristics from the locally experienced crowd onto the abstractly imagined community of mass culture.

But Le Bon's formulations did not reign unchallenged during the modern period. Although the figure of the crowd was often used to malign the lower orders of the class system as hive-mindedly destructive or to assert their manipulation by a massified culture, it also provided a conceptual tool to render the new experience of urbanization. For example, in King Vidor's film *The Crowd* (1928), the crowd acts as a generic antithesis to the domestic sphere. In an early title card, protagonist Johnny Sims is advised: "You've got to be good in that town if you want to beat the crowd." This crowd-as-competition motif is reinforced in a sequence of shots featuring the city's human density that expand to the scale of the city's imposing skyscrapers, one of which gives way to an interior view of a massive Taylorized workplace in which Johnny's desk is but a speck in the crowded room. For Vidor, the crowd is an abstraction of the urban experience that only exists as an implicit counterpoint to the domestic sphere.

And at a further allegorical remove, the crowd provided both avant-garde and popular writers a figure with which to imagine possibilities for flattened, truly democratic social bodies. When the child David Schearl is electrocuted by the third rail in the climax of Henry Roth's *Call It Sleep* (1934), a crowd of onlookers comes to the rescue. Roth presents a cacophony of disembodied voices representing the many dialects of New York's Lower East Side: "W'at?" "W'ut?" "Va-at?" "Gaw blimey!" "W'atsa da ma'?" they cry out as they discover David's body on the rails (419). In this case, the distinctive traits of the crowd are its diversity and its cooperation, as it collectively finds a broom and arranges David's rescue from the tracks. The effect is twofold: Roth's crowd rejects the stereotypically destructive behavior of so-called crowd mentality, and its coordinated efforts gesture toward a bridging of ethnic dispersal that might only be performed in the networked environment of the crowd. The integrated heterogeneity of the crowd marks it as a social formation that renders each individual on a leveled plane, relating to one another by interpersonal mediating links instead of defining relationships according to social institutions such as, in the case of *Call It Sleep*, ethnicity. So although representations of the crowd often connote the vacuity and viciousness of a mythic crowd mentality, they also carry a utopian charge, positing a field in which individuals are freed from institutional social barriers to create links of their own design.

The six-degrees-of-separation theory, purportedly only a convention of postmodern narrative, provided the modernists with another register for representing their networked milieu. Indeed, there is a direct line of continuity between the modern and postmodern uses of the six-degrees narrative: the focus on characters' chance crossings, on the varied strengths of ties between them, on the contingent nature of the entire diegesis of the text—these are common not only in 1990s and 2000s film but also in modern fiction. This is the organizing principle in, for example, Dos Passos's *Manhattan Transfer* (1925), in which the "transfer" is not a rail station but the myriad exchanges that take place among the novel's dozens of characters as their lives intersect, entangle, and diverge. It is a strategy Dos Passos also deployed throughout the fictional narratives of his *U.S.A.* trilogy, as the fourth chapter discusses in further detail. The six-degrees model of social networks offered modernist writers a means of rethinking the physical boundaries of a knowable community, as well as the degrees of intimacy needed to maintain it, as a vital response to the rapidly urbanizing, globalizing world.

From collage in the visual arts to the crowds of modernist fiction, the use of network figuration is intuitive. Without our informational vocabulary—or for that matter, a frank announcement of network aesthetics or politics that would have suited the modernist genre of manifesto writing—the moderns never registered their experiments in the language of networks. Nevertheless, these modernist projects anticipate the networked patterns and principles that would rise to prominence in the theory and representation of the digital revolution, globalization, and postmodernity. In other words, studying the networks of modern thought, experience, and aesthetics is not an anachronistic application of contemporary paradigms backward onto texts that have little use for them. Rather, this study illuminates an archaeology of network discourses—a range of representational models that have fallen by the wayside somewhere during the middle of the twentieth century—that demonstrates gaps in our contemporary narrative and theory. Reading modernist narrative for these abandoned conceptions of networked space demands in turn that we reformulate our basic understanding of the cultural logic of modernism.

Networks of Modernism

The continuity of six-degrees narratives in both modernist and postmodernist narratives prompts a return to the stakes of *Networks of Modernism*. The continuity of this particular mode of network aesthetics is in fact a marker of the broader *dis*continuity of network devices between the modern and postmodern periods. In other words, out of the array of network devices in modernism—the formal interplay of fragment and totality, the treatment of crowds and public spaces, and the exploration of six-degrees formations—postmodern narrative seems to have narrowed the spectrum of networks to an either-or proposition between the six-degrees theory in fiction and film and the hypertextual narratives of digital environments. Bordwell's *Poetics of Cinema* (2008) draws on previous studies of "thread structure" and his earlier designation of the "network narrative" genre to position texts such as Robert Altman's *Short Cuts* (1993) and Quentin Tarantino's *Pulp Fiction* (1994) as an expression of the six-degrees theory.[19] For Bordwell, the network is bound to this narratological convention and cannot expand beyond its limit. In *Reading Network Fiction* (2007), David Ciccoricco studies hypertextual narrative. "Network fiction," he writes, "makes use of hypertext technology in order to create emergent and recombinatory narratives" (4). Ciccoricco uses this framework to study the nonlinear organization of texts such as Michael Joyce's *afternoon* (1990) or Judd Morrissey's *The Jew's Daughter* (2000), which can only exist in electronic form. "Network narrative" and "network fiction"—these genre classifications reflect not a failure of scholarly perception, but a very real contraction of the range of network devices in the passage from modernist to contemporary narrative. And they should give scholars of modernisms pause to reevaluate the truly unique interventions of the interwar period.

Whereas Bordwell and Ciccoricco delimit the conventions of a network genre, I consider modern American narrative's broad range of engagement with the urgent dialectical tensions of totality and fragment, unity and dispersal. Whether in distributed form or in content that establishes networks of people, goods, and technology, the texts I have selected for study challenge the narrow confines of today's narrative production and also provide markers of the limitations of contemporary theory that invoke networks. It is this breadth of network aesthetics that allowed modern narrative to confront the myriad complexities of the period, reformulating national space and theorizing social configurations with the full scale of modern experience in view. To follow the assumption that networks belong solely to the postmodern is to forfeit this crucial dynamic of the moderns' intellectual and aesthetic production.

But even while I stake out the discontinuities of network aesthetics in the shift from the modern to the postmodern, the driving tension of the modern experience offers some continuity with the late twentieth and early twenty-first centuries. After all, the network is the defining feature of poststructuralism, a handy figure for rejecting the binaries of structuralism that are so often associated with the modern period. Some might argue, however, that a dominant trait of the postmodern is the primacy of the fragment, which is stripped of an attendant impulse to totalization—for example, in its treatment of entropy or its rejection of the grand narrative. But postmodernism is also typified by totalizing gestures, as demonstrated by Fredric Jameson's cognitive mapping or Agamben's vigorous study of globalization across the humanities or the smooth space of singularity.[20] So whether within a single text or across an entire period of intellectual and aesthetic production, the dialectical tension of fragment and totality signals a residual trace of modernism within the postmodern. This trace marks the modern in the network genres studied by Bordwell and Ciccoricco as well as the network discourses of Deleuze and Guattari, Hardt and Negri, the digital humanities, and so on. It is a trace inflected to account for the digital revolution and transformations in globalization, but a trace that nonetheless shows the interpenetration of these two periods of intellectual history. In other words, the persistence of the cultural logic of modernism—the dialectic of fragment and totality and its mediation by the network—makes networked discourses of the postmodern period articulable.

The following chapters reassess the possibilities of network aesthetics as they manifested in modern American narratives spanning the canonical and noncanonical, the avant-garde and popular. The texts I study—Randolph Bourne's "Trans-National America," Jean Toomer's *Cane*, Anita Loos's *Gentlemen Prefer Blondes* (1925), John Dos Passos's *U.S.A.* trilogy, and Nathanael West's crowd fiction, particularly *The Day of the Locust* (1939)—demonstrate a range of network configurations that these writers used to think through the crises of the period. But they also track a narrative of decline for the network, beginning with Bourne's brand of utopian optimism for distributed social space and concluding with West's fiction, which so roots the radicalism of networks in modern experience that the figure could only contract in its usefulness to contemporary aesthetics and theorists.

From this grouping of writers, one should not infer that there was a discernible coterie of moderns practicing, theorizing, and promoting these aesthetics. Indeed, of the myriad informal schools of modernist production, there is no "networkism" to speak of. And even if there were such school to affiliate with, it would be fair to wager that these writers would have found each other's aesthetics and politics disagreeable. The public intellectual Randolph Bourne was known among his friends for his magnanimous spirit, but he could never manage to stay in the good graces of editorial staffs for long, and he quite painfully broke with his mentor John Dewey over his wartime dissent. Jean Toomer famously spurned any form of artistic affiliation, even rejecting association with the Harlem Renaissance before giving up on the project of creative writing altogether. Herself a staple in the celebrity press, Anita Loos traveled mostly in Hollywood circles, and her few sustained ties to the literati involved H. L. Mencken and F. Scott Fitzgerald. Dos Passos eulogized Bourne in *1919* (1932), the second volume of his *U.S.A.* trilogy. But Dos Passos's political enthusiasm during the 1920s and 1930s would have made for tension alongside the ambivalence of Toomer or Nathanael West, to say nothing of Loos's latent conservatism. West, an enigmatic persona of nearly continuous self-fashioning, had several ties to fellow moderns as coeditor of the little magazine *Contact* and through his visits to the Greenwich Village bohemians, but out of a mix of shyness and contrarianism he kept mostly to himself. To put it bluntly, a cocktail party putting these writers into close contact would not have been a pleasant affair; sustained contact through an informal salon would have been an absolute train wreck. But the array of these authors is instructive, reflecting the wide range of perspectives that employed networked models across the field of modernist narrative. In other words, these chapters map out the constellar quality of the American moderns' use of networked representation, and the juxtapositions and lacunae created by the incongruities of the authors and texts give this project a quality similar to one of modernism's aesthetic hallmarks, collage.

Before offering close readings of modernist narratives that deploy such networked organization, chapter 1 offers a study of the 1910s public intellectual Randolph Bourne's direct, heavily political, and euphoric use of the network thinking that would be adopted in later modernist aesthetics. A progressive, a vocal opponent of the United States' entry into World War I, and a culture critic at large, Bourne wielded great direct and indirect influence over many of the moderns who would seek new models of community in a nation that no longer held the promise of cohesion. In fact, through their mutual friend Waldo Frank, Bourne's understanding of distributed space was transmitted to Jean Toomer as he was revising *Cane*. Bourne's essay "Trans-National America" announces the failure of the melting pot—a failure that had been in the offing well before the war began but that was more or less completed as the Great War took Europe and threw the United States into a disarray of divided national loyalties. During the preparedness debates, two major discourses arose in response to the waning of the melting pot and the beckoning call of the Great War: on one hand, an Americanism that retrenched the melting pot's rendering of a homogeneous, unified nation; on the other hand, a pluralism that recognized ethnic diversity and understood national space as a diasporic landscape of discrete cultural centers. Bourne responds to these discourses with a call to readjust the very meaning of Americanism, proposing a "federation of cultures" that would transform the ethnic enclaves into nodal communities comprising the network of America. Against Americanism's homogeneity and pluralism's dispersal, this distributed, federated organization of cultures would be "the great American democratic experiment," he wrote (117). Bourne offers no qualifications or reservations in celebrating his thesis, upholding his distributed vision of space as a solution to crises of national identity at home and even for conflict deterrence abroad. Bourne's political model failed to take root in the 1920s, overrun by the rampant nativism and xenophobia of the interwar years. But his networked model of national community nevertheless persisted in much of the moderns' aesthetic production as they continued to struggle with the defining tensions of the period, and the utopian note to Bourne's formulation would transfer to Jean Toomer in a crucial period of his work on *Cane*.

Chapter 2 studies the formal architecture of Jean Toomer's *Cane* as an experiment in networked organization that presents an allegorical rendering of race in America. Comprised of thirteen short stories, fifteen poems, and a longer segment verging on drama, *Cane* presents readers with serious interpretative dilemmas, not the least of which is taxonomy. It is clearly not a novel in any conventional sense, and the formal diversity of its texts excludes it from being called a short story cycle. Yet its title suggests something more coherent than a mere collection of assorted works, and Toomer expressed reluctance to let the pieces stand alone, writing of anthologies such as *The New Negro* (1925): "I did not want *Cane*, which is an organism, dismembered, torn to bits and scattered about in the pages of anthologies" ("This May Be Said" 102). Critics have often discussed *Cane*'s textual unity in terms of hybridity, but the stubborn independence of Toomer's stories and poems defies any attempt to think of *Cane* as a sort of textual fusion. Instead, *Cane* allows the autonomy of these texts and their interdependence through a network of repeated phrases and figures that bridges *Cane*'s lacunae, creating a spatial dimension for the text's formal interplay. This shift from hybridity to network also prompts a new reading of Toomer's social poetics. Drawing on Bourne's zeal for the network, *Cane*'s form allegorizes the distributed situation of race relations in the United States, imagining this new mode of social space as a resolution for the cultural and racial tensions the text represents.

Turning from the avant-garde to the popular, chapter 3 focuses on Anita Loos's *Gentlemen Prefer Blondes*, studying how it stages public settings as sites of radically distributed space. Loos's novella was the second-best-selling work of fiction in the year following its publication, and it created a franchising juggernaut that banked on its success. *Blondes* rode to success mostly on the back of protagonist Lorelei Lee, known for her inadvertent wit, her extravagant flapper lifestyle, and the suggestions of her promiscuity. The novella also addresses the period's crises in social organization through Loos's use of the grand hotels that are Lorelei's haunt of choice—settings that foster social networks and undermine class hierarchy. Despite having priced out the vast majority of the American public, grand hotels had a reputation as public spaces because their lobbies, bars, parlors, ballrooms, and restaurants were freely accessible to any reasonably dressed white person. For this reason, historian A. K. Sandoval-Strausz frames the hotel as a contact zone in which locals and travelers mixed in the hotel's public spaces. It is precisely this connective element of the hotel that Lorelei uses to forge links to people from an array of nationalities and class positions. Acting as a dominant hub of social networks that she creates around her, Lorelei, ever the social climber, flattens class hierarchy into a constellar organization. Perhaps inadvertently, Loos offers a restructuring of the class system that eschews the stratification of caste in favor of a more entangled, networked social arrangement akin to a cocktail party—another of Lorelei's, and Loos's, favorite spatial-social sites. In this light, and despite Loos's own conservative politics, *Blondes* poses the network as a utopian formation against class hierarchy.

Chapter 4 returns to the study of modernist formal experimentation with an analysis of John Dos Passos's *U.S.A.* trilogy. Like *Cane*, *U.S.A.* defies traditional literary taxonomy. The trilogy traces the history of the United States from 1900 up to the late 1920s and the onset of the Great Depression, displacing linear narration in favor of four separate modes of representation that Dos Passos thought would more accurately communicate the spirit of the times. This narrative architecture, which Dos Passos referred to as a "four-way conveyor system," is comprised of four independent narrative mechanisms: Newsreel passages that use newspaper copy, advertisements, and song lyrics to capture the zeitgeist of the period; Camera Eye passages that narrate the lived experience of the period through a stream of consciousness based loosely on Dos Passos's own life; biographical sketches that outline the period through portraits of leading figures such as Woodrow Wilson, Andrew Carnegie, and the Wright brothers; and fictional narratives that illustrate the period through a matrix of twelve primary characters experiencing different events and developments of the early 1900s. *U.S.A.*'s narrative system makes a constellation of its own form, linking these autonomous elements so that they cooperate to narrate the crises of the modern period. This system reflects the networked organization of Fordist production, perhaps explaining Dos Passos's description of the trilogy as a "conveyor system." The formal ar[illegible] produces two schisms in the corpus of modern networ[illegible] these ruptures takes place within *U.S.A.*'s understanding of the subst[illegible] networks. Prioritizing distributed schemas to narrate the period rather than linear trajectories, Dos Passos applies networks to the study of history—and thereby signals a step away from the radical revisions of national and social space that were the focus of earlier works of network aesthetics. Meanwhile, there is friction between the trilogy's formal architecture and the content of its fiction, which features a six-degrees landscape of characters. This friction creates a second rupture, which points toward the displacement of formal experiment by an ascendant six-degrees schema. These schisms make visible some of the shortfalls of contemporary network aesthetics, which, typified by Bordwell's "network narrative genre," relies almost exclusively on the six-degrees model.

The final chapter examines representations of crowds and the masses in Nathanael West's fiction, particularly *The Day of the Locust*. Noted for its climactic scene of a rioting crowd, *Locust* is but a part of West's career-long interest in the signification of crowds. The chaotic finale of *Locust* belies the nuance of West's engagement with crowds. It is easy for some to read West as a direct descendant of Le Bon, as *Locust*'s climax seems to confirm Le Bon's worst fears of the crowd's hive-minded barbarism. But the rowdiness of the climax, reflective of the unruly audiences of the nickelodeon era that loom large in the background of this Hollywood novel, overshadows the simple facts of West's configuration of crowds. Rather than the homogenous mass one would expect to find in such representation, West's crowds are internally diversified: they expand according to the logic of networks rather than assimilate the individual into an undifferentiated mass. Although crowds were a popular subject for West and his contemporaries because of their association with urbanization and fascism, they also appealed to the moderns because their distributed organization provided a means of rethinking the nature of democracy during its crises in the period. West's crowds are radical in their opposition to massified fascism, but they also punctuate a narrative of decline for modern network aesthetics. West's emphasis on the innately public body of the crowd contrasts with Bourne's focus on the enclave's autonomy, marking a shift in perspective of the moderns' treatment of the network from the node to the [illegible]llar system. But because [illegible]n experience of the [redacted] [illegible] s radical reorganiz- [redacted] hitecture, however, [illegible] buted treatment of [redacted] aesthetics. One of [illegible] l, West's fiction sets [redacted] postmodern contraction to the [illegible] and hypertextual fiction. *Locust* marks not only the limitations of contemporary network aesthetics but also a shortcoming in today's networked discourses, which seem largely unable to imagine collectivity growing out of connectivity.

1

In Lieu of a Manifesto

Randolph Bourne's "Trans-National America" as an Origin of Network Aesthetics

As he was preparing to return from his Grand Tour, just after having observed nationalist demonstrations in Dresden on the day Austria declared war on Serbia, Randolph Bourne wrote to his friend Alyse Gregory: "there is an interesting prospect in the way of a new radical paper dangling tantalizingly before my eyes. My intransigent reputation, though, is going to damage, I think, my chances of getting any very permanent position." Indeed, his tenure with the *New Republic* would prove to be rocky and short—just as it would with the *Atlantic* and *Seven Arts* throughout the middle and late 1910s. Whether for a congenital intransigence or an ingrained will to dissent, Bourne's inability to sustain good relations with editorial staffs for long fits a broader narrative of his experience on the margins. He broke with his former teacher John Dewey over the perversion of pragmatism to support the war effort. His interests in culture and aesthetics led him to the bohemian scene of Greenwich Village, but, as Christine Stansell details in *American Moderns* (2000): "he was too much of an unknown for the likes of Mabel Dodge or the Hapgoods" and instead circulated in the lesser known Patchin Place salon (216). Above all, his radical critique of the Great War, its preparedness campaigns, and its anti-German fervor set Bourne at odds with the American mainstream so much that writing assignments were increasingly hard to come by. Hunchbacked from the age of four by a case of spinal tuberculosis and bearing the facial deformities of what he would later describe as a "terribly messy birth," he carried the modern tropes of alienation and the grotesque in his very body. A tragic pariah, at 32 a casualty of the 1918 influenza pandemic, Bourne would be mythologized by later moderns such as John Dos Passos.

Bourne's lack of a social network—or more specifically, his lack of steady affiliation with one of the informal cadres that dotted the modern landscape—

left him alienated not only from his peers but also from his legacy in the scholarship of American modernism. Unlike other intellectuals of the period, Bourne is perceived not to have an immediate association with any of the signal projects of modernism, not even the pageant theater or "sociological" fiction that so interested him. Throughout the middle 1910s, Bourne secured a reputation as a public intellectual through his writing on Deweyan education and the generational identity of youth—a reputation that declined in inverse proportion to his increasingly passionate dissent from the Great War and that continues to define the scholarship on Bourne today. But while other public intellectuals, such as Du Bois or Freud, offer readymade inputs to a discussion of modernist innovations such as the New Negro or stream of consciousness, Bourne's influence has proven elusive to scholars of modernisms.

This treatment of Bourne's legacy devalues his signal intervention into the cultural logic of modernism. Although there is no overt statement of "networkism" among the myriad manifestos of the period—no program to rival F. T. Marinetti's 1909 declaration of futurism, the announcement of vorticism in *BLAST* in 1914, Mina Loy's "Feminist Manifesto" of 1914, and so on—Bourne does this work by proxy. His article "Trans-National America," published in the *Atlantic* in July 1916, celebrates a distributed understanding of national space to negotiate the diasporic effects of immigration and the homogenizing discourses of Americanism and preparedness, as well as the uniformity of a massified culture. He situates the network as a utopian political model for managing these prewar ruptures in national identity. Whereas Stein's *Three Lives* (1909), discussed in the introduction, poses an even earlier register of modernist networks, the overt nature of Bourne's expository writing charts a more systematic or codified methodology of distributed thinking. Although "Trans-National America" does not directly invoke the term "network," its adoption of *unanimisme*, the theory of a networked milieu that Bourne adapted from the French poet and essayist Jules Romains, demonstrates the importance of distributed models to Bourne's essay. This is most prevalent in his vision of a "federated" conception of national space, which would be adopted by his friend and fellow student of Romains, Waldo Frank. Inspired by a poet, Bourne's political thesis would eventually take its place as a surrogate manifesto of network aesthetics, influencing subsequent American moderns' aesthetic experiments both directly and indirectly.

Alongside Bourne's profound marginalization, he maintained an investment throughout his writing in the "Beloved Community"—a term that he adapted from the philosopher Josiah Royce and that would later become a central feature of Martin Luther King Jr.'s politics[1]—marking the cultural logic of modernism not as an abstract dialectical tension but as an experience that Bourne lived perhaps to a greater extent than any other modern American. Bourne's call for a new, networked national identity is at the same time a refashioning of community in this pursuit. As the mass public emerged and began to disrupt conservative assumptions of the knowable community, and as the United States weighed the merits of an identity that lay in a homogenous past or one set in a diasporic future, Bourne recognized that community would have to take a new shape. Although others looked back wistfully to a mythical, preindustrial social whole, Bourne proposed the "federated" space of transnationalism as a flattened, utopian community that would sustain the nation and the globe through the crises of the early century.

Americanism, Cultural Pluralism, Transnationalism

Bourne concludes "Trans-National America" with a call to action that would likely have struck readers as something of a commonplace during the preparedness campaigns. Of his proposed transnationalism, he writes: "Here is an enterprise of integration into which we can all pour ourselves, of a spiritual welding which should make us, if the final menace ever came, not weaker, but infinitely strong" (123). The rather stale preparedness rhetoric of these last lines, however, should not dampen Bourne's major intervention for both the politics and the aesthetics of the modern period. Indeed, "Trans-National America" is an indispensable text for modernist studies because its argument rests on the usefulness of networks in negotiating the period's tensions between fragmentation and totality as they manifested in two political discourses of the prewar years. Americanism and cultural pluralism sought to stabilize a nation in flux, beset by unprecedented rates of immigration into the United States as well as the stressors of the beckoning war in Europe. Behind these tensions, Bourne also addresses the emergence of a massified public that was fundamentally altering conventional understandings of group organization. These prewar discourses were still grappling with the major demographic changes in immigration into the United States, which around 1890 was shifting from the largely British, German, and Nordic populations to new groups—predominantly Slavs, Italians, and eastern European Jews.

As David Goldberg demonstrates in *Discontented America* (1999), by 1910 an increasing number of immigrants came from eastern Europe and the Mediterranean, with the foreign-born constituting some 13 percent of the total United States population and representing as much as 50 percent of some northern cities (141). The arrival of these immigrants heightened xenophobia throughout the preparedness campaigns and the Great War, culminating in the 1924 National Origins Act, which set hardened quotas favoring the more "desirable" nationalities of the pre-1890 immigrants.

To understand the fullness of Bourne's intervention, one must first survey the prevailing discourses of the prewar years. One response to the influx of new peoples was a blanket reassertion of the nation's homogeneity under the aegis of Americanism. Theodore Roosevelt toured the country in 1915 and 1916, advocating war preparedness and national unity with the nativist slogan "100 Percent Americanism." Likewise, Woodrow Wilson invoked the dangers of "hyphenate" voters, particularly German-Americans, during his 1916 reelection campaign (Goldberg 148). Closely attending the nexus of Americanism and preparedness was a renewed investment in Americanization. Frances Kellor, whose *Straight America* (1916) Bourne reviewed for the *New Republic*, was a major figure in this movement. She writes: "*Preparedness means* something more than a larger army and navy. It means also having a united America back of that army and navy" (Kellor 154). Kellor's Americanism emphasizes fusion in service of preparedness but otherwise departs from Roosevelt's nativist and xenophobic brand in calling for progressive projects such as the erasure of illiteracy and the extension of "one American standard of living" to all immigrants (188). "*It means*," Kellor writes, "*putting the American flag* above all others, abolishing dual citizenship, and pledging *open* allegiance to America" (185). Drawing heavily on Kellor, Royal Dixon's *Americanization* (1916) espouses a beneficent, liberal sort of politics. For example, Dixon advocates the "English only" platform to provide the immigrant better access to civil institutions and to protect him from labor exploitation. "The greatest protection that the schemer and slanderer, the rioter, the blackmailer, and the usurer can have," Dixon explains, "is the ignorance of his opponent" (22). Dixon's vision for America, although largely eschewing xenophobic "hyphenate" language, still posits the nation as a unified, homogenous body to which an immigrant could be inducted through English education, Kellor's "Americanization Day" celebrations, and so on.

Bourne never wrote about Dixon, though his papers list *Americanization* among the books he read in 1916. His review of Kellor, however, serves as a response to both writers' shared vision of a homogeneous Americanism. Although he applauds Kellor's avoidance of nativism, Bourne remains concerned that any Americanism program "is almost necessarily nativistic in its implications. It is notorious that the conception of national unity which includes military preparedness, industrial mobilization, universal military service, belligerent defense of American rights, is one held largely by the stanchly nativistic element" ("Americanism" 197). Indeed, it seems that "national unity" is for Bourne itself a shibboleth to be suspicious of. Rather, Bourne writes that the "America and its ideal of the future are still in the making, and that a premature cohesion on a basis of belligerent self-protection would defeat that slow learning to live together which a wise and modern Americanism involves" (197). Bourne's refusal of Anglo-Saxon homogeneity as a "premature cohesion" lies at the heart of his rendering of national space in "Trans-National America."

Whereas proponents of "100 Percent Americanism" and even advocates of a progressive model of Americanization located national identity in a mythic, homogenous past, cultural pluralism emerged during the prewar period to argue for a diverse, even diasporic concept of national space. Horace Kallen would coin the term "cultural pluralism" in 1924, but his 1915 essay for the *Nation*, "Democracy Versus the Melting-Pot," lays out the groundwork of the discourse.[2] Kallen surveys the national space as a striated landscape of disparate cultural centers:

> when we consider that portion of our population which has taken root, we see that it has not stippled the country in small units of diverse ethnic groups. It forms rather a series of stripes or layers of varying sizes, moving east to west along the central axis of settlement, where towns are thickest; i.e., from New York and Philadelphia, through Chicago and St. Louis, to San Francisco and Seattle. Stippling is absent even in the towns, where the variety of population is generally greater. Probably 90 percent of that population is either foreign-born or of foreign stock; yet even so, the towns are aggregations, not units. (192)

For Kallen, this ethnic striation spatializes national identity. He points to Scandinavian, German, Irish, and Jewish enclaves as demonstrations of cultural autonomy practiced in the upper Midwest and throughout urban New England (218). And as further proof of the legitimacy of this pluralist national identity, he locates it within the very Anglo-Saxon tradition that "old stock" Americans venerated as an ideal of homogeneity: "England is a state of four nationalities—the English, Welsh, Scotch, and Irish (if one considers the Empire, of many more), and while English history is not unmarred by attempts at unison, both the home policy and the imperial policy have, since the Boer War, been realized more and more upon the voluntary and autonomous cooperation of the component nationalities" (219–20). Kallen's America flatly rejects the smooth homogeneity of Roosevelt's Americanism, instead locating the nation's strength in its perceived weakness, in its fragmentation.

Bourne intervenes with a truly unique innovation, mediating the two polarities—the homogeneous Americanism of Kellor, Dixon, and Roosevelt and the dispersal of Kallen's cultural pluralism—with a vision of the United States as a networked space. Bourne's "Trans-National America" opens with a cavalier dismissal of mythic homogeneity, holding that of the Great War's many outrages for the American public, chief among them was its achieving the demise of the melting pot metaphor of national identity. To recognize the failure of the melting pot, Bourne writes, "is not, however, to admit the failure of Americanization. It is not to fear the failure of democracy. It is rather to urge us to an investigation of what Americanism may rightly mean" (108). The crises of prewar America, he suggests, called for a new understanding of social coherence and a recalibration of the projects of Americanism and Americanization. "America is a transplanted Europe," Bourne writes, "but a Europe that has not been disintegrated and scattered in the transplanting as in some Dispersion. Its colonies live here inextricably mingled, yet not homogeneous. They merge but they do not fuse" (114). Mingled but not homogeneous, balancing dispersion and fusion, Bourne's understanding of American social space clearly hails—and denies—the discourses advanced by Kellor and Kallen. Rather than shoehorn these diverse populations into an idealized fusion, Bourne proposes "a clear and general readjustment of our attitude and our ideal" so that it better aligns with the real, lived space of prewar America (108).

I want to pause to reflect on this phrase—"they merge but they do not fuse"—because it highlights the intervention of Bourne's transnationalism. Of course, on one plane this program negotiates Americanism's demand for unity and cultural pluralism's insistence on the preservation of traditional identity categories. Whereas Kallen's cultural pluralism asserts the virtues of fragmentation, Bourne's "readjustment" instead posits a truly radical rearticulation of community, American space, and of the experience of modernity. This "readjustment" rejects the outdated models of fusion and identity and instead operates on the principles of a distributed network. He acknowledges the entrenchment of "clusters" of immigrants, but instead of merely following Kallen's thesis of striated ethnic enclaves, Bourne casts these clusters as nodes that are the fundamental units of a distributed—not an atomistic—landscape (108). The distributed logic of transnationalism is such that this first, domestic plane opens onto a second, global plane: the first renders a constellation of ethnic traditions within the United States; the second renders a constellar relation between the United States and the globe. Indeed, these two planes are interdependent and often intersectional in Bourne's transnationalism thesis.

Bourne's intervention lies not only in transnationalism's relations to the discourses of the preparedness campaigns but also in community formations as they are conceived in the postmodern age. To the extent that Bourne's transnationalism manifests residually in today's discourses of postmodernity and globalization, its nodal character is often outweighed by smoothened, totalizing social formations. One such example is the recent discussion of singularity, which in *The Coming Community* (1993) Giorgio Agamben describes in two ways. On the one hand, it is a method of thought that is "freed from the false dilemma that obliges knowledge to choose between the ineffability of the individual and the intelligibility of the universal" (1). On the other hand, this singularity is also an object, creating a social formation that "form[s] a community without affirming an identity" and "rejects all identity and every condition of belonging" (86, 87). Although the first description has a distributed quality, the second emphasizes homogeneity—especially in Agamben's removal of the identity formations that Bourne so diligently sought to preserve. This is the distinction between Bourne's transnationalism and Agamben's singularity: one gets that sense that Agamben advocates a community that "fuses without fusing."

The language of "federation" is critical to understanding the distribution inherent to transnationalism.[3] Although the term and its derivatives connote organization of the state, Bourne uses them in their generalized sense to describe a form of community that allows autonomy of its parts while still asserting their interdependence—if not necessarily their unity. "Federation," in other words, signals "network" organization. For Bourne, writing before the digital age would introduce a vocabulary to parse the different modalities of networks, the language of federated statehood had to suffice to explain the distributed model he was advocating. For example, in light of massification's erosion of a "distinctively American culture," Bourne writes: "It is apparently our lot rather to be a federation of cultures" ("Trans-National" 115). He uses similar language to describe an alternative to cultural pluralism. Instead of failing at the project of the melting pot, Bourne writes: "What we have achieved has been rather a cosmopolitan federation of national colonies, of foreign cultures, from whom the sting of devastating competition has been removed" (117). Bourne's assertion of "federated" national space may also respond to Kellor, who in arguing for a homogeneous Americanism calls for a correspondingly unitary state to supplant the United States' federal arrangement. Scrutinizing the citizenship procedures that in 1916 varied by state, Kellor asks: "Of what possible value can state and district lines be in a national citizenship matter? Are we a nation or are we a conglomeration of states and districts?" (98). Bourne's answer to the second question is a paradoxical "yes." By positioning the United States' domestic dynamism as cooperative and not competitive, as federated and not merely fragmentary, Bourne extends the federalist arrangement of the nation's government to its social organization. In doing so, he decentralizes the authority of an Anglo-Saxonist melting pot and sets the cultural dominant on a flattened, distributed plane with precisely the ethnic enclaves that so threatened "100 Percent Americanism" advocates such as Roosevelt.

At the same time, Bourne's interdependent federation provides a more integrated model of the nation than Kallen's disparate cultural pluralism. Indeed, in its nodal configuration, Bourne's "federation of national colonies" closely resembles the "stippling" spatialization that Kallen rejects in favor of striation. Whereas Kallen's striations situate cultural centers in absolute parallel, Bourne's "federated" language emphasizes intersection and interpenetration. And as Leslie Vaughan argues in *Randolph Bourne and the Politics of Cultural Radicalism* (1997), Bourne rejects not only Kallen's formulation of national space but also his rendering of personal identity. "Like his friend Kallen," Vaughan writes, Bourne "believed that identity was a product of the given 'place,' that is, the regional, traditional, and familial determinants of a people (descent); but he also recognized that identity was manifested in willed attachments to others (consent) through affiliations in 'communities of sentiment'" (130). If anything, then, Bourne considered cultural pluralism a point of departure for his transnationalism thesis.[4] But in ultimately refusing Kallen's essentialist identity and allowing for affiliation, for consent as well as descent, Bourne establishes a new model for the interconnections of personal identity and the social sphere. For Bourne, the distributed network of ethnicities, cultures, and traditions lies at the heart of "the great American democratic experiment" ("Trans-National" 117). The network, in other words, was for Bourne the fundamental organizing principle of modern American life.

The readjustment Bourne advocates, replacing the homogeneous melting pot with a distributed understanding of the nation, is informed largely by the work of Jules Romains. In addition to Bourne's "federation" language, Romains's influence is critical to recognizing the networked composition of transnationalism. Romains posited the literary and theoretical concept of unanimisme in a 1905 manifesto for the French literary journal *Le Penseur* and again in his book-length poem, *La vie unanime*, in 1908. This framework, which asserted the networked configurations of the social milieu, gave rise to a school of young French writers referred to as unanimistes. In March 1914 during his Grand Tour, Bourne met Romains, who furnished him copies of his books,[5] and among Bourne's journal from 1916–18 is a list of "Unanimiste Works" that he was either reading or setting aside for future reference. Bourne was not affiliated with the unanimiste cadre, but Romains's language nevertheless colors much of his writing and illuminates the distributed logic of his transnationalism thesis.

Unanimisme, a neologism drawing on the French *unanime*, which translates as "unanimous," characterizes the milieu as a network comprised of individuals and technology—what today Romains might refer to as the interrelations of the human and the nonhuman or perhaps situate in the field of actor-network theory. It is a fundamentally urban, material formulation. As Rosalind Williams explains, Romains's poetic epiphany arrived at rush hour: he saw the street, the teeming crowd, the passing vehicles, the shops lining the thoroughfare all together as a coordinated body—itself but one iteration of a larger "elemental being" (185). Williams describes Romains's work as being invested in the network of daily living: "He is the poet of urban systems, . . . fascinated by the new ways of living and feeling he saw developing along with new systems of communication and transportation. The dominant technological presence in unanimiste poetry is the subtle pattern of city vehicles weaving an ever-changing yet predictable network" (179). If this were Romains's only accomplishment, he would be a fertile enough source for studies in the literature of science and technology. But more instructive for scholars of modernisms, and what Bourne found more useful in his work, is Romains's intervention to mediate the cultural logic of modernism. The unanime—the basic unit of study, such as the rush hour streetscape or a public plaza such as Washington Square in Greenwich Village—encompasses the individual's relation to the group in a discrete space. Williams argues that unanimisme, the recognition of interconnection at the site of the unanime, is fleeting and place-specific, but nevertheless it negotiates Romains's desires for individuality and solidarity by granting the individual autonomy from the crowd (194). In other words, Romains outlines a sociological theory that emphasizes interpenetration and interdependence rather than an either-or proposition between fragmentation and homogeneity.

As a negotiator of the modernist dialectic, Romains proved useful for much of Bourne's work. Bourne wrote about Romains in the posthumously published essay "A Sociological Poet," in which Romains is upheld as "a Whitman industrialized" and "the poet of the crowd" (522, 523). Bourne is less interested in Romains's theory of the milieu in the essay than he is in his formulation of a social identity, writing that unanimisme is "the group-life of the city, the surge of the mass" (523). Surveying several of Romains's poems, Bourne finds the contours of this "group-life" highly flexible. At times, unanimisme subordinates individual experience to a monolithic social form. In the crowd, Bourne writes, "the individual is dissolved" (524). But unanimisme is also the networking device that bonds individuals while still holding them distinct. It is the study of the group as it is "all mysteriously linked by this subtle social force" and as it stages "the whole drama of individual and society" (525). This formulation of group-life also appears in another posthumously published piece, "Pageantry and Social Art," which describes the 1910s experiments in pageant theater—especially the 1913 Paterson Strike pageant—as works of "group-art," displays of "group-talent," and outbursts of "group-emotion" (516–19). Although the unanimiste language of "Pageantry and Social Art" is unattributed, Romains's imprint—alongside Bourne's formulation of unanimisme as "group-life"—is unmistakable. Indeed, it permeates Bourne's thinking.

Although "Trans-National America" does not display "group-life" language, the essay nevertheless demonstrates the contours of unanimisme as Bourne understood it. Bourne transforms the investment in "group-life"—the networked mediation of individual and the crowd—from the localized scene of the unanime to the scale of national space. In other words, Bourne's focus on "group-life" broadens unanimisme from its rendering of a place-specific community to the imagined community of the nation. Bourne unbinds Romains's rush hour streetscape and locates the ethnic group as the basic unit of interconnection, using Romains's template to link the nation's and even the globe's manifold identities into a flattened plane. Bourne suggests this unanimiste interplay when he describes transnationalism as the negotiation of "two colossal constellations of states" (122), referring to the Allied and Central powers. By invoking the networked composition of the constellation, Bourne posits a utopian formulation of groups that transcends place and provides an adaptable model for treating the tensions of the modern period.

The national "group-life" is at stake when, with a typical polemical flourish, Bourne assails the Americanism and Americanization campaigns for being slavishly devoted to "English Kultur," calling attention to their antidemocratic model of assimilation at the same time that he suggests a note of the iniquitous "hyphenate" even among the stalwart Brahmins. And to further demonstrate the inadequacies of a homogeneous model of Americanism, he points to the South as its truest expression. The South "is culturally sterile," Bourne writes, "because it has had no advantage of cross-fertilization like the Northern states" (112–13). This characterization has the disadvantage of being largely untrue—given the South's population of African Americans to whom Bourne is mostly blind—but it provides a sharp bogeyman for the "Anglo-Saxonizing" thrust of Americanism.

In the course of denouncing "English Kultur," Bourne touches on another index of the modern pull toward homogenization: the massification of culture. Whereas a fully realized "English Kultur" inevitably degrades the entire nation to the level of the backwards South, Bourne finds the homogenizing effects of mass culture equally deleterious, producing "masses of people who are cultural half-breeds, neither assimilated Anglo-Saxon nor nationals of another culture" and leading to "the cultural wreckage of our time" (113, 114).

The heart of the problem, Bourne writes, is the lowest-common-denominator nature of Americanization: "It means that, letting slip from them whatever native culture they had, [immigrants] have substituted for it only the most rudimentary American—the American culture of the cheap newspaper, the 'movies,' the popular song, the ubiquitous automobile" (113). Bourne's use of "culture" suggests the term's fuzziness, connoting anthropology in Kellor and Kallen and aesthetics in the lament of movies and Tin Pan Alley.

In "Masscult and Midcult," Dwight Macdonald locates the continuity between Americanization and mass culture in Bourne's investment in the Beloved Community. The Beloved Community is one manifestation of Bourne's lifelong study of "group-life," as he understood it.[6] The common problem of Americanization and massification, according to Macdonald, is erasure of the knowable community, which for Bourne posed an existential threat to the sustainability of group-life. "Since in a mass society people are related not to each other but to some abstract organizing principle," Macdonald explains, "they are often in a state of exhaustion, for this lack of contact is unnatural" (23). For Macdonald, the problem is the same in crowds, which have no intrinsic identity, but are only perceived as groups in relation to an external referent or perspective. Macdonald asserts that these twinned group formations, mass and crowd, motivated Bourne's work because they enervated any possibility of community by this externalization. He concludes that massification renders a pluralistic society impossible (34). Given the failures of Americanization and mass culture to create a community worthy of the "beloved" descriptor, Bourne indeed decides that "there is no distinctively American culture" and rejects the premise of any Americanism or Americanization project as Kellor, Dixon, or Roosevelt would have had it ("Trans-National" 115).

Macdonald tidily demonstrates the through-line of Americanization and massification in Bourne's work, but it would be a mistake to follow his conclusion that Bourne found a better model of community in cultural pluralism or that he found it at all desirable as a solution to the crisis of national identity. Indeed, the distributed model of unanimisme was so persuasive for Bourne that it informed his thoughts about personal identity as well as national space. In "Old Tyrannies," a posthumously published fragment written in 1918, Bourne invokes the term "network" in addressing the binary of descent and consent: "We live almost entirely a social life, that is, a life as a constituted unit in society, rather than a free and personal one. Most people live a life which is little more than a series of quasi-official acts. Their conduct is a network of representations of the various codes and institutions of society" (171). Indeed, for Bourne the modern self is a social text, as Ross Posnock rightly argues in "The Politics of Nonidentity" (1992). Posnock situates Bourne in an intellectual genealogy alongside Henry James, John Dewey, Theodor Adorno, and Michel Foucault, who all in diverse ways strain against homogenizing systems of thought. Posnock reads Bourne's oeuvre as committed to an agential irony that "engages in public life and upholds intellectual responsibility while resisting conventional modes of engagement and responsibility" (42)—perhaps one explanation for the refusal of affiliation that Bourne feared would be perceived as "intransigence." Although the determinism of "Old Tyrannies" seems to reject the consent of affiliation that he allows in the formation of community, Bourne's assertion of a distributed subject in the essay does not merely provide an analogue of his transnationalism thesis. Rather, a cosmopolitan, networked self—one that incorporates the determinants of place as well as "willed attachments to others"—is the discrete building block of transnational space.

Bourne proceeds to situate the United States' networked domestic space as a model for the broader project to distribute global space across a network as well. He locates the United States' "federation of cultures" as a local iteration of the spatial experience of modernity itself:

> America is already the world-federation in miniature, the continent where for the first time in history has been achieved that miracle of hope, the peaceful living side by side, with character substantially preserved, of the most heterogeneous peoples under the sun. Nowhere else has such contiguity been anything but the breeder of misery. Here, notwithstanding our tragic failures of adjustment, the outlines are already too clear not to give us a new vision and a new orientation of the American mind in the world. (Bourne, "Trans National" 117)

The cosmopolitanism inherent to this "world-federation" is demonstrated by the young, modern American.[7] For Bourne, the network's mediation of homogeneity and dispersal, of fragment and totality provides hope not only for the American project but for the international one as well. The American experiment is but one node on the global network: "America is coming to be, not a nationality but a trans-nationality, a weaving back and forth, with the other lands, of many threads of all sizes and colors" (121).

The key to both of these distributed spatial schemas is a recuperation of the hyphenate. "Dual citizenship we may have to recognize," Bourne writes, "as the rudimentary form of that international citizenship to which, if our words mean anything, we aspire" (119). Bourne would develop this claim further in "The Jew and Trans-National America," an address he delivered to the Harvard Menorah Society in late 1916 and subsequently published in the *Menorah Journal*, in which he argues that such dual citizens were the nation's salvation, having prevented entry into the Great War (125). Bourne appeals in the essay to newly appointed Justice Louis Brandeis as a hyphenate whose patriotism was beyond reproach and casts Jewish dispersion as the condition of the modern—in other words, as an expression of the cultural logic of modernism. Indeed, for Bourne the hyphenate is crucial to transnationalism because a hyphenated America and a hyphenated globe would effect conflict deterrence: "A trans-nationality of all the nations, it is spiritually impossible for [the United States] to pass into the orbit of any one. It will be folly to hurry herself into a premature and sentimental nationalism, or to emulate Europe and play fast and loose with the forces that drag into war" ("Trans-National" 122).

Bourne's radical networking of American and global space still falls short of its own expansive logic, as several of his critics have noted. Vaughan, for example, writes that Bourne's transnationalism accommodates only European immigrants and finds his silence on matters of race striking (136). Indeed, the opening paragraph of "Trans-National America" orients his argument only toward the assimilation of Germans, Scandinavians, Bohemians, and Poles. And even Bourne's Eurocentrism is not entirely egalitarian, suggesting a residual hierarchy of ethnicity: "I do not mean that the illiterate Slav is now the equal of the New Englander of pure descent. He is raw material to be educated, not into a New Englander, but into a socialized American along such lines as those thirty nationalists are being educated in the amazing schools of Gary" (109). It is this same exclusion of racial identity that allows Bourne to misrecognize the cultural—and thereby ethnic and racial—homogeneity of the South. His recognition of group-life, in other words, is at best incomplete.

Bourne's vision of America remains radical, however, in its transcendence of the binaries that so often underlie crisis. Later moderns would adopt this transcendence as a logic of representation. In relation to Bourne's investment in the Nietzschean framework of the Apollonian and the Dionysian, Vaughan characterizes him as unwilling to resolve opposites into synthesis, setting him apart from the tendencies of progressives and radicals of the prewar years (4). Vaughan traces this approach through Bourne's refusal of false choices:

prowar and antiwar, American and immigrant, poet and critic, and so on (5). His use of irony to address such polarities, she writes, "left contradiction alone, untranscended, expressing different possibilities and different experiences of social truth" (52). Across Bourne's prolific output, spanning some 1,500 articles, Vaughan's reading bears out. But in the case of "Trans-National America," Bourne instead favors the dialectical. Kellor's Americanism and Kallen's cultural pluralism are not contradictions to be left "untranscended." Rather, they are polarities to be mediated, to be "federated." They pose antitheses that must be made antinomies. Such was the lived experience of the hyphenate. Such was the promise of the American experiment. Indeed, for Bourne the promise of an American cultural tradition was that it lay paradoxically in the future: "As long as we thought of Americanism in terms of the 'melting-pot,' our American cultural tradition lay in the past. It was something to which the Americans were to be molded. In the light of our changing ideal of Americanism, we must perpetuate the paradox that our American cultural tradition lies in the future" ("Trans-National" 115).

In its drive to mediate and federate binaries, Bourne's transnationalism also challenges identity—not personal or national identity, but identity as a homogenizing system of thought. Indeed, Bourne's constellar space and distributed subject mediate the antimony of identity and difference. Posnock's study of "the politics on nonidentity" situates Bourne in a tradition that "encourage[s] our suspicion of categories, including those of intellectual and political identity   oppositional, radical, liberal, conservative. One could say that the Frankfurt motto *nicht mitmachen* (not playing the game) also becomes the creed (or anticreed) of Dewey after the First World War and of his student Bourne in 1915" (38). Adorno's antisystem of negative dialectics exemplifies Posnock's genealogy. Bourne shows his commitment to nonidentity, Posnock writes, in his reflections on pragmatism and his crafting of the public intellectual's role in political crisis—both of which faced major stressors in the preparedness campaigns and in the Great War. In these terms, however, Bourne's transnationalism does not merely preserve "the nonidentical, the particular" from being devoured by an identity in which "unlike things become alike," to paraphrase the programs of Posnock's nonidentity thinkers (37). Rather, Bourne's transnationalism celebrates the interpenetration of unlike ethnic positions to create a national space that is neither uniform nor fragmentary and in doing so celebrates dialectics—an open dialectics that, in its expansive and adaptable form, avoids the pitfalls of closure and finality that led Adorno to negative dialectics. In other words, Bourne's transnationalism achieves an alternate configuration of "nonidentity." Its network does not resolve or synthesize the antinomy of identity and difference as it manifested in the modern tensions of unity and dispersal. But in mediating these tensions Bourne proposes a social space that can withstand the crises posed by each polarity and that situates distributed social organization as the utopian "miracle of hope."

Toward an Aesthetics of Transnationalism

Of course, Bourne's transnationalism would be foreclosed nearly as soon as he asserted it. The United States' entry into World War I, some nine months after the publication of "Trans-National America," emboldened nativist sentiment and shattered any potential of a peaceful "world-federation." Even after the war and its preparedness rhetoric had subsided, Woodrow Wilson scapegoated immigrants for his own failure to lead Congress to ratify the Treaty of Versailles in 1919, suggesting that "the most un-American thing in the world is a hyphen" (Goldberg 24). Indeed, the debates over a homogeneous Americanism and cultural pluralism would not be settled by the Great War. The early 1920s featured a resurgent Ku Klux Klan, and the 1924 National Origins Act made a policy of xenophobia by resetting immigration quotas in favor of Anglo-Saxon and Nordic ethnicities while curtailing the entry of Eastern Europeans and Asians. In this political climate, Bourne's vision of a constellar, distributed national space simply withered on the vine.

Although Bourne's network failed to take hold of the political sphere, it provided many subsequent moderns with a device for apprehending the modern milieu, particularly for negotiating the aesthetic polarities of fragment and totality that typify modernist experimentation. To put it in Posnock's terms, transnationalism's politics of nonidentity would give rise to a poetics of nonidentity, acting effectively as a manifesto of network aesthetics. Bourne did not pioneer this field alone, as earlier experiments such as Stein's *Three Lives* or the collage inventions of Picasso and Braque in 1912 or several other avant-garde modernist projects could attest. But Bourne's essay is unique in its expository demonstration of network dynamics, and it would influence later modernist aesthetic experiments at least partly because of its origins in Jules Romains's literary theory and poetry. In some cases, that influence would be surprisingly direct.

Bourne's understanding of unanimisme's "group-life" spread into modern aesthetics in large part through his friendship with Waldo Frank, who enacted Bourne's networked "clusters" schema in *Our America* (1919) and translated unanimisme into fiction in *City Block* (1922). *Our America*, a product of exchanges of cultural envoys between the United States and France during World War I, takes up the work of defining American culture to a foreign audience. Bourne biographer Bruce Clayton argues that *Our America* was influenced by another of Bourne's essays, "The Puritan's Will to Power," published in 1917 in Frank's little magazine *Seven Arts* (236–37). But it is "Trans-National America" that undergirds Frank's formulation of distributed national space, which displaces the traditional centrality of the country's Puritan inheritance by articulating a new American culture as it is perceived by "the younger generation"—the "our" of the title. Frank echoes Whitman's multitudinousness in describing this culture: "America is a complex of myriad lights playing upon myriad planes. . . . Its reality is but a sprawling continent—mountains and gardenland and desert—swarmed by a sprawling congeries of people. To bound it is to stifle it, to give it a definite character is to emasculate it, to offer it a specific voice is to strike it dumb" (*Our America* 8). The project, in other words, is not only the displacement of the Puritan tradition, which could very well be accomplished by installing in its place another dominant cultural center, such as industrialism. Instead, Frank aims for a fully distributed arrangement of American cultural space.

To articulate this decentralized, multitudinous conglomerate of cultural traditions, Frank draws on the nodal patterning of ethnic enclaves that his friend Bourne had set out in "Trans-National America," displacing the monolithic legacy of Puritan New England with a network of cultural centers. Frank's distributed cultural centers gesture toward the diversity of American cultural inheritance, spanning the spatial, ethnic, literary, and generational dimensions of American culture. He provides a close study of New England, the Native American southwest, Chicago, and New York, as well as the contributions of Jewish Americans, Whitman, and the young generation to the multivalent constitution of American culture. For Frank, this mixture results in a "Whole" even as it disrupts conventional chains of genealogy.[8] Whereas Bourne's network of identities and affiliations is mostly a matter of the present, a cosmopolitanism that was already being lived and that could lay the groundwork for a fruitful future, Frank's network of clusters extends to the past. His "Whole" rejects the linearity that would draw a straight, uninterrupted line from the Puritans to twentieth-century America. Frank's America maps over a web of disparately threaded cultural legacies, providing a new dimension for Bourne's thesis of a "federated" culture.

Frank also shared an investment in Romains—and especially Bourne's reading of unanimisme. Bourne and Frank, who along with Van Wyck Brooks and Lewis Mumford made up the group loosely referred to as "Young America," sought to establish Romains's reputation in the United States. Frank's *City Block*, a short story cycle featuring some dozen characters who live on the same block in varying degrees of awareness of each other, takes Bourne's understanding of the "group-life" implicit in Romains's essays and poems and applies it to fiction. Frank, whom Mark Whalan characterizes as a good friend of Romains's, was so invested in unanimisme that the little magazine *S4N* dedicated two articles of its January 1924 edition to Frank's work with the concept (194). And Gorham Munson's 1923 study of Frank's oeuvre suggested that *City Block* would inaugurate "an American phase of *unanimisme*" (53). As Casey Nelson Blake argues, however, Frank was skeptical that the French underpinnings of unanimisme could not map out directly onto the United States, particularly warning against a literal importation of Romains's project that would take for granted an "inherited language of culture and morality" that more typified French traditions (146). "Starting from such a premise," Blake continues, "American writers would end up as apologists for the existing industrial order. Nonetheless, Romains remained a model for Frank of a prophet of a new culture, 'one in which the newly organized individual would create the transfigured group'" (146). Frank, with his use of a "federated" culture in *Our America* and his narrativization of unanimisme in *City Block*, is the clearest manifestation of Bourne's influence on the moderns. Frank also, as will be seen in the following chapter, is the intermediary between Bourne and Jean Toomer, whose experiment with distributed form in *Cane* was influenced by Bourne's work as well as Romains's, and whose networked space provides a fuller dimension of race than Bourne's Eurocentric transnationalism. Frank and Toomer are the most visible links of a wide-ranging influence that set Bourne's utopian theory of networked national space at the center of modern American fiction.

It is not surprising that Bourne's political manifesto would lay the groundwork for later modernist projects. Feeding the moderns' zeal for the new,

Bourne's outline for a new model of ethnic and national identity would prove adaptable to a variety of aesthetic experiments. The strength of its appeal lies in its promise of a new mode of the Beloved Community—one that for Bourne could answer to the crises of national identity that roiled the preparedness campaigns, and could respond to the distinct noncommunity introduced by massification. For later moderns, starting with Frank and Toomer, the distributed model could be adapted to suit a variety of frictions in modern social space. Casey Nelson Blake argues that Bourne's commitment to the Beloved Community is largely a romantic critique of industrial capitalism, and that its transnationalism thesis poses little more than a "secular jeremiad" forging regeneration out of the past (120). Blake writes that Bourne and his fellow Young America thinkers vacillated between "technocratic social engineering" on the one hand and "purely aesthetic solutions to political problems" on the other (6). This characterization often holds in Young America writing, but not in Bourne's transnationalism thesis, in which he imagines the Beloved Community as neither nostalgic nor homogeneous. In "Trans-National America," he explicitly situates retrospection as the impulse of a conformist Americanism: "All our idealisms must be those of future social goals in which all can participate, the good life of personality lived in the environment of the Beloved Community. No mere doubtful triumphs of the past, which redound to the glory of only one of our trans nationalities, can satisfy us. It must be a future America, on which all can unite, which pulls us irresistibly toward it" (123). Bourne discards any notion of nostalgic unity in favor of a new mode of national community that demands full participation, doing away with any presumptions of mythical wholeness and face-to-face relations in favor of a grand, distributed social scheme.

Bourne's network of America shows its truly utopian impulse in this essay. This impulse is not without its own contradictions, however. On the one hand, Bourne modeled the transnationalism thesis on the lived experience of the present. In this sense, his call for "a clear and general readjustment of our attitude and our ideal" of Americanism was meant to reconcile the ideal with the cosmopolitanism that was already being lived. On the other hand, transnationalism was very much the scaffolding of the future—not only a reconciliation to the present but a template for a social organization that remained a horizon. The friction between the presentness and futurity of transnationalism is one of the most productive attributes of Bourne's essay. It demonstrates that although the project of transnationalism is far from complete, it is a horizon that is rather modest by the standards of the utopian tradition. To put it in the terms of Ernst Bloch's *The Principle of Hope* (1954–59), Bourne's transnationalism resembles a concrete more than an abstract utopia because it is already seeded in history rather than being derived without due consideration to the limitations of the present. Whereas later modern aesthetic projects would deploy this figure largely to allegorize social space, for Bourne the network of transnationalism was a blueprint for a lived community that was tantalizingly close.

To be sure, subsequent moderns would take that blueprint in a variety of directions. The following chapters chart out shifting perspectives on such organization: Bourne and Toomer emphasize the autonomy of a network's subordinate units, but in Nathanael West's fiction crowds grant more attention to the fusion of the whole, aligning more closely with the singularity that "fuses without fusing." In this range of experiments, the possibility of merging without fusing at the very least presents, to borrow Blake's phrase indicting the utopian elements of the Young America thinkers, an aesthetic solution to the aesthetic problems of fragment and whole. But also—and despite Blake's wariness—the emergence of distribution in Bourne's manifesto and in modern American aesthetics poses the utopian virtue of "purely aesthetic solutions to political problems." Indeed, to the extent that Bourne's program was still equal parts abstract and concrete, it is a utopian project that demands allegorical figuration in order to imagine a social organization that could survive the tensions of the modern period. It is a project, in other words, that could imagine how it is that the units of a transnational nation could "merge but . . . not fuse." This feature—the federation that is both abstract and concrete and that promises to stabilize the binaries of the period's manifold crises—might well announce the projects of American modernism.

2

Network Form as Network Politics in Jean Toomer's *Cane*

Before his spiritual awakening to Gurdjieffianism beginning in the mid-1920s and to Quakerism in the late 1930s, Jean Toomer's creative output in the early 1920s was typified as much by its extraordinary experimentation as by his contrarian posturing. His rows with Alain Locke, the figurehead of the Harlem Renaissance whom Toomer had consulted early in the drafting of *Cane* (1923), are the most symbolic of his refusal of affiliations. For instance, he was enraged that Locke published his one-act play "Balo" in his anthology *Plays of Negro Life* (1927). Toomer recalls having submitted the piece to Locke and Thomas Montgomery Gregory "years before" but did not consent to its publication: "They had done nothing with it. I had forgotten I had written it. I had forgotten they still had it. Imagine my surprise, then, and my anger years later suddenly to see this naïve attempt appearing in a collection" ("This May Be Said" 103). Of course, several literary historians have argued that it was not the publication of an unformed piece that angered him so much as an unwelcome association with the New Negro. As is routinely observed, the very project that would bring Toomer into circulation was the one for which he held the deepest scorn. Indeed, until his spiritual turns, Toomer repudiated any association that would situate him in a network of relationships, especially those involving identity groups or the moderns' informal schools of aesthetics. When he did cultivate a relationship, it was strong but relatively short-lived—as demonstrated by Waldo Frank, who provided key editorial advice during the writing of *Cane*—and rarely led to a broader array of ties. But despite Toomer's refusal of social networks, *Cane* marks a significant achievement in modernist experimentation precisely because its form relies on networked figuration and uses distributed models to reimagine the meaning of race in interwar America.

Like many works of high modernism, *Cane* demonstrates paradoxical impulses in its reliance on formal fragmentation and its insistence on the totalization of its component parts—a tension mapping over the cultural logic of modernism. Toomer's most famous and lasting work, *Cane* is situated between two interwar paradigms for understanding race and ethnicity that correspond closely to this dialectal tension: the residual attachment to the melting-pot model of national fusion and a rising emphasis on nativism and the atomization of identity groups. *Cane* mediates this polarity with its distributed organization—both in its network of form comprised of short stories, verse, and a dramalike section, and in the circulation of the eponymous commodity, cane, throughout its content. Reading *Cane*'s repetition of phrases and figures as the linkages of a textual network not only enables readers to resolve some of the text's formal challenges but also to see how network aesthetics facilitated Toomer's reengineering of American social space.

Drawing on Randolph Bourne's political manifesto of distributed space as it was adapted into narrative by their mutual friend Waldo Frank, Toomer follows with a politically engaged network aesthetics. The crises facing the two writers are similar, as are their responses. Bourne engages the prewar discourses of immigration, which privileged either a homogeneous Americanism or a diasporic cultural pluralism, with the federated space of nodally construed ethnic enclaves. Toomer intervenes in the interwar discourses of race and ethnicity—which in radical cases advocated a melting-pot model akin to *mestizaje* or, more often, endorsed the segregation codified in Jim Crow laws—with a formal allegory for a network of American race. *Cane* is unique in its engagement with the modern period's signal tensions among fragment, totality, and network on the ground of high modernism: form. In this nexus of form and politics, Toomer's work offers a utopian vision of Americanism against the crises of national and racial identities.

Networks of Form, Networks of *Cane*

Composed of thirteen short prose pieces, fifteen poems that include sonnets, ballads, and work songs, as well as a longer piece that nods toward the conventions of drama, *Cane* presents a number of challenges with its form—not the least of which is taxonomy. The dominant trends today are to treat it as a collection or as a short story cycle, but these rubrics are inadequate for Toomer's formal experiment. "Collection" suggests a miscellaneousness that ignores the text's logic of interplay. "Short story cycle" precludes a significant amount of the text dedicated to verse and suggests some narrative conventions—a concrete plot, a common setting, and so on—that *Cane* does not deliver. To follow J. Gerald Kennedy's provision for a short story sequence, which emphasizes the genre's "unfolding and cumulative effects" (vii), poses still another problem in imposing a linearity on *Cane* that precludes a good deal of its spatialized dynamism. Above all, the short story label persists, perhaps because the short story cycle was a staple of modern narrative, as discussed in the introduction. Many such texts would have prepared readers for the kind of work performed in *Cane,* and two of that number—Sherwood Anderson's *Winesburg, Ohio* (1919) and Waldo Frank's *City Block* (1922)—were major influences specifically cited by Toomer.

In the failure of these taxonomies, I situate *Cane* amid the moderns' experiments with network aesthetics. Given the interplay of its component texts, along with the interchanges of commodity circulation that take place in its content, *Cane* may be best understood when read as a network of forms—perhaps even as an intensification of the distribution that already informs the short story cycle. It is an ideal case study in American modernism's development of network figuration because it relies on its connective tissues to an unparalleled extent, offering no place, no character, no plot, not even a consistent form, but only a logic of patterning and repetition that endows its several texts with nodal relationships to each other. To read *Cane* in such terms foregrounds not only how these component texts illuminate each other but also how the gaps that take place between them create meaning in negative space. And because it recognizes the text's spatial dimension, the network model is also better suited for understanding Toomer's major interventions in rendering national space.

The strategies of *Cane*'s networks lie in the crossroads of its form and its content, both of which are famously fragmentary. Like many modernist texts, *Cane* tries to have it both ways at the formal level by asserting a host of fragments at the same time that it tries to totalize them into a unified system. And like many modern works, *Cane* mediates these two polarities with networks. This design is clear from Toomer's objections to having his pieces appear as excerpts in anthologies.[1] He allowed segments of *Cane* to appear in three anthologies of black writers throughout the 1920s, and a few pieces circulated in various anthologies from 1927 to 1969 while *Cane* itself was out of print. But

Toomer was generally reluctant to allow the pieces to stand alone. Demonstrating his general repudiation of anthologies, Toomer accused Alain Locke of printing the short story "Fern" in *The New Negro* (1925) without his consent. As he wrote of the many requests from editors, "I did not want *Cane*, which is an organism, dismembered, torn to bits and scattered about in the pages of anthologies" ("This May Be Said" 102). The tensions between Toomer and these editors underscore the interdependence he intended to build among the different texts of *Cane*.

One key way that Toomer achieves this networked interconnection of texts is what many scholars, drawing on visual metaphor, refer to as collage. Indeed, collage is a dominant term in *Cane* scholarship because it protects the text from the dismemberment of the "organism" that so worried Toomer. As noted in the introduction, collage is an umbrella term for many techniques—including papier collé, assemblage, decoupage, photomontage, and montage—that have in common an aesthetic of fragmentation that creates meanings in the interstices of different images and materials. Collage, writes Jean-Jacques Thomas, results in "the establishment of new networks of significance" (80).

Relying on the networked logic of collage, *Cane* effectively posits a distributed system of literary forms. Not only does it integrate prose pieces, verse, and a quasi-dramatic element into its networked system, it also suggests that these forms themselves are often internally unstable. "Beehive," for example, has the surface values of a sonnet: fourteen lines with a turn registering between the octave and the sestet, where the focus changes from the beehive of urban density to the speaker, a drone longing for freedom. But it rejects any conventional meter or rhyme scheme in favor of free verse: "Wish that I might fly out past the moon / And curl forever in some far-off farmyard flower" (50). Some readers might be tempted to view "Beehive" as a local illustration of the text's overall hybridity, in its blending of a traditional form such as the sonnet with the more modern element of free verse. But instead the poem illustrates collage's principal of juxtaposition, which, rather than hybridity, is the fundamental logic of *Cane*. The poem's most productive technique is to juxtapose these two poetic modes—the sonnet and free verse, the traditional and the modern—to establish its "network of significance," one that finds its locus of meaning somewhere between these traditions.[2]

"Beehive" is but one case study of the principles of collage guiding the text. The juxtaposition of *Cane*'s various poems and short stories in the first two sections underscores the networking of the text by establishing text-to-text, node-to-node relationships that are the ligatures of *Cane*. In other words, these intertextual relations are the lines by which *Cane* marks its formal networking schemes. To achieve this distributed form, *Cane* relies on the repetition of figures and the gaps creating space between those repetitions. For example, Karintha, the eponymous subject of *Cane*'s first story, is described as being "as innocently lovely as a November cotton flower" by a preacher who catches her at mischief (3). The second poem of the text, "November Cotton Flower," develops the flower to configure the first section's schema of autumnal imagery that laments the passing of the rural way of life (6). There is no vulgar equation of Karintha to the flower of the poem, but the repetition of the image creates a line between the short story and the poem—a relation that has nothing to do with likeness, so much as it foregrounds the dynamic interplay of texts.

Toomer deploys the same strategy of textual interplay through the figure of the wayward son. "Song of the Son," the fifth poem and eighth overall piece of *Cane*, features a speaker returning to the ancestral land of the South to remember the songs of slaves, lest he forget "What they were, and what they are to me" (14). The narrator of "Fern," the short story separated from "Song of the Son" by the poem "Georgia Dusk," is a similar figure, who observes to himself: "I was from the North and suspected of being prejudiced and stuck-up" (17). And both Ralph Kabnis and Lewis, of the concluding quasi-drama "Kabnis," are perceived as outsiders because they have come to Sempter, Georgia, from the North. Again, the repetition of the figure of the wayward son establishes connections across *Cane*. The figure does not create a dominant theme or even a motif for the text but underscores the interconnections of its component parts.

The intertextual elements are perhaps most striking in the juxtaposition of "Portrait in Georgia" and "Blood-Burning Moon," the last two pieces of the first section of *Cane*. "Portrait in Georgia" is a free-verse poem that depicts a woman's face in the language of lynching, describing her hair as "coiled like a lyncher's rope" and her body as "white as the ash / of black flesh after flame" (29). This first reference to racial violence in *Cane* is immediately followed by a deeper exploration of that theme, insofar as "Blood-Burning Moon" concludes with the grisly lynching of Tom Burwell by a mob of "white men like ants" (35).

Critics often describe these interstitial, intertextual sites of meaning-production as lacunae—purposeful gaps in the text, say, between the lynching thematics of "Portrait in Georgia" and "Blood-Burning Moon." The meanings created in these interstices vary according to the subject and the arrangement of the texts that span the gap. In the case of the pair of lynching pieces, the intervening lacuna could signify something like the unspeakability of the atrocity—a hushed reluctance to narrate the event that later falls over Ralph Kabnis as his friends Fred Halsey and Professor Layman discuss local iterations of racial violence in the third section, "Kabnis." It is equally important to observe how these lacunae shape a spatial organization of *Cane*. By inscribing these open spaces between pieces, Toomer reinforces the spatial figuration of the network in *Cane*'s very form. The work is defined as much by its nodal interconnections as it is by the vast gaps spanned by the nodes' relational lines. The spatial nature of *Cane*'s network again suggests its similarity to the visual form of collage, which deploys lacunae, or negative space, between juxtaposed images to stretch out the relationships of incongruous images across the field of vision.

Although collage defines *Cane*'s connective formal strategy, there remains a good deal of networking material in the content of Toomer's stories and poems. The first section of *Cane* establishes something akin to six-degrees networks for three figures: King Barlo, Old David Georgia, and an anonymous woman. Barlo appears as a traveling companion of the narrator in "Becky," the object of young Esther's desire in "Esther," and the subject of one of Tom Burwell's passing remarks in "Blood-Burning Moon." Old David Georgia is named as one of the townspeople who support the exiled woman in "Becky," and he reappears as a gossipmonger around the cane-processing stoves in "Blood-Burning Moon." Similarly, an unnamed woman is the subject of brief discussion in "Fern" and "Esther" for having drawn the Madonna on a courthouse wall. In each case, a series of appearances suggests a six-degrees formulation of the social landscape in the first section, which is all we have to establish the connective logic of that section because its setting is not continuous across the various texts. This mode of networks, however, cannot hold the entire text of *Cane* together because there is no overlap of characters between the rural setting of the first section and the urban milieu that follows in the second.

In the absence of any kind of knowable community in the urban settings of Washington, D.C., and Chicago, the second section focuses more on the material, technological mediations that facilitate networks. "Her Lips Are Copper Wire," for example, is a free-verse poem depicting a technologically mediated romance in which the woman on the other end of the phone line is part love interest and part personified mechanization. Her body *is* the technology that conveys her voice. Although her lips double as the "copper wire" of the phone line itself, she becomes a cyborglike figure in the closing lines: "then with your tongue remove the tape / and press your lips to mine / till they are incandescent" (57). She must "remove the tape"—presumably electrical tape—that binds her wire-lips in order to embrace the speaker and electrify him too with a kiss. Toomer imbues this fundamental human interaction with a quite literal charge of electricity, drawing both the woman and the speaker into an exchange that is simultaneously romantic and technological.

"Kabnis," the third and final part of *Cane,* argues for a historical mode of connection. This is a mostly linear model of connection that links Father John, the deaf-mute whose experience bears witness to the days of slavery, to the young generation of Ralph Kabnis, who himself is deaf to Father John's testimony. Father John testifies, "O th sin th white folks 'mitted when they made the Bible lie," but Kabnis, having already taunted the old man repeatedly, only glares back at him with a look described as "contemptuous" (117). The generational disjuncture is obvious, but this exchange is most noteworthy for the way Toomer poses a challenge to readers to recognize this transgenerational network where Kabnis fails to see it.

The most important networking device in the content of the text, however, is cane itself. And in choosing sugarcane as the motif for this task, Toomer, of course, selected a burdened feature of African American history and experience—both in its broad contours and in the specific moment of *Cane*'s writing and publication. Alongside cotton and tobacco, the agricultural labor of sugarcane is one of the decisive markers of black oppression across the Atlantic, particularly the southeast of the United States. In addition to evoking the hardships of the antebellum and Reconstruction periods, sugarcane also signals more specific experiences of sharecropping that Toomer would have observed during his travels through the South as he was drafting *Cane.* As David Goldberg explains in *Discontented America,* sharecropping was already established as a defining experience of Southern African American life by 1900, operating on a system of "debt peonage" in which landowners supplied the sharecroppers with durable and consumable goods at a high rate of interest that resulted in a state of servitude-by-debt (93). And it was hard, hard labor, defined more by the hoe and the mule-drawn plow than the mechanized agriculture that was becoming prevalent in the North (106). The interwar period saw these deprivations worsen. Prices for crops, which had risen throughout the war years, simply bottomed out in the early 1920s. As Mark S. LeClair shows in his study of commodity markets, the sugar market was hit particularly hard. In 1920, a pound of sugar fetched as much as eleven cents, and by 1925 the price had dropped just below three cents (LeClair 72). An influx of sugar from Cuba during the same period only exacerbated the problem for American sharecroppers. These conditions fueled the Great Migration and exacerbated labor conflicts that were already dire, having manifested in the Red Summer of 1919.[3] Those who remained sharecroppers during the 1920s would face an increasingly desperate challenge to work harder and harder in order to eke out a meager living.

In this fraught moment, sugarcane does unique work for the text. Cane is not simply an image that repeats in all three sections of the text in the way that images of dusk and autumn repeat in the first section to advance its narrative of decline. Rather, cane is a commodity that circulates in the text. In charting that circulation, I offer a rudimentary exercise in text mining to follow the patterns of cane, which in turn provide a mode of connection that supplements the networked logic of *Cane*'s form. Charting the flow of a particular commodity is a means of sketching the lines of a network, as in the flow of wheat in Frank Norris's *Epic of the Wheat* cycle. There, the transmission of wheat links the struggling farmers of central California to each other in *The Octopus* (1901), connects the farmers to the Chicagoan stock traders and speculators of *The Pit* (1903), and draws the farmers and speculators into connection with starving wheat consumers of Europe in the planned but unwritten finale to the trilogy, *The Wolf*. In this way, Norris sketches connections among southern California, Chicago, and Europe, demonstrating the interdependence of individual characters who have never met but who share a concrete interest in wheat, the material mediation of their network. Of course, the commodity does not need to be a crop to perform this narrative function, but Norris provides a handy demonstration of this material device in the scale of his distributed epic.

Toomer's commodity of choice carries far heavier symbolic import than Norris's, and its signification varies across the three sections of the text. A study of these uses of cane demonstrates how the commodity creates a distribution of form and content across *Cane*. When indexing each occurrence of cane in the text, one notices that its uses can be loosely categorized according to the section of the text in which it appears. In other words, a general schema of cane signification typifies each section. Accordingly, the sectional uses of cane draw networks for each discrete section of the text, and its circulation across all three sections draws a network for the whole of *Cane.*

In the first section, where cane appears most frequently and diversely, the commodity acts as a place-specific image of work and community. Cane first appears in "Becky," the story of a white woman marginalized from town for having and raising two black sons, as one of the offerings brought to Becky by the townspeople who support her in exile. "Old David Georgia, grinding cane and boiling syrup, never went her way without some sugar sap," the narrator observes (8). In its first use, cane acts as a commodity that maintains Becky's ties to her estranged community. In "Carma," the story of the woman who fakes her suicide in order to deceive her lover, cane is a figure of portent in the story's epigraphic poem: "Wind is in the cane. Come along. / Cane leaves swaying, rusty with talk, / Scratching choruses above the guinea's squawk, / Wind is in the cane. Come along" (12). In the ballad "Georgia Dusk," cane demonstrates the synchrony of man and agriculture with images such as the "cane-lipped throng" inscribing cane onto the very faces of the workers or with sounds such as the singing of cane that rise above the fields: "Their voices rise . . the chorus of cane" (15; the two-dot ellipsis is Toomer's). In "Fern" and "Blood-Burning Moon," the canebrakes offer a place of concealment for sexual rendezvous between the narrator and Fern and between Louisa and Tom Burwell (19, 30). In the free-verse poem "Portrait in Georgia," it is the one image of beauty to counterbalance the atrocious language of lynching used to describe the woman's appearance: "Breath—the last sweet scent of cane" (29). In addition to its place as sexual rendezvous for Louisa and Tom Burwell, cane has two appearances in "Blood-Burning Moon." We see it being processed by Old David Georgia in the text's only scene of cane-related labor, and it is onto this scene that Bob Stone stumbles to learn of Louisa's indiscretions with Tom (31, 34). The metaphorics of cane can be manifold, evocative of sweetness, fecundity, sexuality, and even violence. It does not act as a stable, unifying image of textual coherence. Instead, I understand the diversity of jobs it performs as a system working—much in the fashion of the networked form of the text—autonomously and cooperatively to root these characters in their rural community, in the agricultural labor that sustains it, and in the system of labor exploitation evoked by both. In this way, cane codes the legacies of slavery while also signaling the very present hardships of sharecropping in the early interwar years.

Set in the urban milieus of Washington, D.C., and Chicago, the second section deploys cane as a figure of nostalgia for an imagined, idealized community of the South. In "Theater," John dreams that Dorris uses the scent of cane to mark herself as "down home": "Of old flowers, or of a southern canefield, her perfume" (55). In "Calling Jesus," it is a substance of comfort to the wayward woman of the sketch, who winds up "cradled in dream-fluted cane" (58). In "Box Seat," cane is a marker of class, as down-and-out Dan is quick to note: "I was born in a canefield" (59). It appears in the Whitmanian free-verse poem "Harvest Song," in which the speaker, a reaper whose repetitious "hunger" marks a desire for the simplicity of an agrarian past, remarks: "It would be good to hear their songs . . reapers of the sweet-stalk'd cane, cutters of the corn . . even though their throats cracked and the strangeness of their voices deafened me" (71; the two-dot ellipses are Toomer's). Finally, in "Bona and Paul," cane acts for Paul as an image of an imaginary and idealized Southern community:

> Paul follows the sun to a pine-matted hillock in Georgia. He sees the slanting roofs of gray unpainted cabins tinted lavender. A Negress chants a lullaby beneath the mate-eyes of a southern planter. Her breasts are ample for the suckling of a song. She weans it, and sends it, curiously weaving, among lush melodies of cane and corn. Paul follows the sun into himself and Chicago. (73)

In the second section, cane acts in a more predictable, thematically oriented pattern. Often manifesting in or associated with dreams, it marks a nostalgic look toward the community and ways of living from the rural South that characterize the first section. At the same time, the metaphorics of cane in this narrative of nostalgia and collective memory may well distort the very community it looks back to. For the nostalgia for cane in this section relies precisely on *forgetting* its contexts of oppressive agricultural labor and the violence that accompanied it, during both the history of slavery and the miseries of sharecropping that marked the interwar period. It is only as a sanitized commodity that cane can perform this nostalgic function, and in streamlining its meaning from the variable uses in the first section, the second section's patterns of cane demonstrate just this act of forgetting.

For "Kabnis," the third section set in the small town of Sempter, Georgia, Toomer attributes to cane a vocal quality, first appearing in contrast to Professor Layman: "Layman's voice is uniformly low and soothing. A canebrake, murmuring the tale to its neighbor-road would be more passionate" (92). Shortly thereafter, Toomer reinforces cane's vocal capacities: "The countryside is ashen, chill. Cabins and roads and canebrakes whisper" (93). As Kabnis flees what he wrongly presumes to be a lynch mob, cane flanks his path, becoming an image of oppression: "A splotchy figure [Kabnis] drives forward along the cane- and corn-stalk hemmed-in road" (93). In its final appearance, cane is again vocalized, this time in the service of night's songs: "Night throbs a womb-song to the South. Cane- and cotton-fields, pine forests, cypress swamps, sawmills, and factories are fecund at her touch. Night's womb-song sets them singing" (105). Murmuring, whispering, and singing, cane's ability to speak deepens the importance of the community dynamics it underscores in the first two sections. In the third section, its vocalization means that it can testify to the history and the present that have emerged around sugarcane.

The payoff of this basic mining of cane usages arrives in its display of the patterns of cane that typify each separate section and that provide an index of network devices in the text's content. For the patterns we see in each section are distributed networks operating on the variable uses of the term "cane." The first section is more diverse in cane's metaphorics than cane's uses in the second section or in "Kabnis," but the breadth of patterns across the entire text shows how truly distributed the use of cane is. Tracing these patterns across all three sections of the text—as a marker of community, as nostalgia for a disappearing and forgotten community, as vocalization of a community's history and its present—also shows how its circulation throughout the text crafts a narrative for *Cane*. Indeed, the network of cane narrates the decline of one way of life, the rise of another, and the testimony of that passage of history. It is common enough to read *Cane* as lamenting the passing of rural Southern communities and customs—or perhaps in light of the specific pressures on sharecroppers in the early 1920s, as witnessing a new phase of misery and desperation in this history. But demonstrating that this narrative is performed in the various appearances of cane shows that the circulation of this commodity also undertakes this narrative in a decidedly distributed organization.

Even aside from this particular narrative of cane's networks, in the diversity of these examples cane becomes a material networking agent that links the people, places, and practices of the text by its very circulation. In *Cane*, the eponymous commodity circulates in such a way that it draws relational lines between some of the elements of the text that are the hardest for readers to assemble, complementing the text's formal networking scheme with a network that operates at the level of content. Cane crosses boundaries of form, appearing in Toomer's short stories, verse, and the drama-novella "Kabnis." It traverses the limits of the urban and the rural, in Georgia, in Washington, D.C., in Chicago, and in the small town of Sempter. Cane is, in short, the material held in common throughout this book, and its very presence connects the text's diasporic forms, characters, and spaces.

The material nature of this connective strategy demonstrates part of Toomer's debt through his friend Waldo Frank to the French poet and essayist Jules Romains, whose literary and theoretical concept of unanimisme is a system comprised of exchanges between material technology and human subjects that places subject and object into a node-network organization.[4] Toomer's networking device is far less new and technological than Romains's reliance on bridges, trains, automobiles, and barges, but he shares Romains's focus on a materiality that brings people, commodities, and place into a distributed system. Indeed, this tie to Romains deepens the critical legacy of *Cane* and charts the links of influence that stem from Randolph Bourne's surrogate manifesto for modern network aesthetics. Critics routinely locate Anderson's *Winesburg, Ohio* and Frank's *City Block* as major influences on Toomer as he was drafting *Cane*. Toomer nodded to both as mentors,[5] and recent criticism has found that Frank had a hands-on role as Toomer's editor. In *Jean Toomer and the Terrors of American History* (1998), Charles Scruggs and Lee VanDemarr explain how Frank—the Pound to Toomer's Eliot—had his fingerprints all over the manuscripts of *Cane*: "Frank selected and critiqued pieces, influenced the ideas and forms for individual stories, suggested at least the theoretical conception for the book's structure, and edited the text line by line" (109). In 1922, the two traveled south to Spartanburg, South Carolina, together as they researched their work. During this period, Toomer was working on *Cane* while Frank was setting the groundwork for the novel he published in 1923 under the title *Holiday*. It was Frank, not Anderson, who ultimately provided Toomer with contacts in the publishing world, advising Toomer about which little magazines to send his poems and short stories to and setting Toomer up with his own publisher, the leading modernist press Boni and Liveright, which published *Cane* in the fall of 1923.

The contrasts between Anderson's *Winesburg, Ohio* and Frank's *City Block* are informative of the networked logic of *Cane*. Both are short story cycles: *Winesburg* is a set of twenty-five stories set in a fictionalized rural town in Ohio, and *City Block* is a set of fourteen stories of people living in the same block in New York City. In terms of aesthetic form, they might bear equal influence on Toomer's reliance on disparate texts coordinating in the absence of a unified plot, character, or even setting. The fundamental difference is that *Winesburg* thematically insists on the atomization of its characters, whereas *City Block* suggests a totalizing vision of its figures. Both works are populated with characters who feel desperately isolated, and convincing readings of *Winesburg* can argue for the interrelationships of Anderson's characters based on their common experiences of existential dilemmas or through the narration of George Willard. *City Block*, however, makes its own case for connecting its various characters, starting right away with its epigraph: "The author assures the reader that City Block is a single organism and that its parts should be read in order" (6).[6] Thus, Frank insists that his stories not be taken as miscellany but read as part of a system. Frank's system hinges on the order of sequence, but even that form allows for interconnections reaching further than the gaps between adjacent stories, thereby creating a totalizing network superimposed over the base sequence driving the reader through the text. *Cane*'s network of form is more fully distributed than the centralized network of *City Block*, in which the connective lines run directly through the character Paolo Benati. Nevertheless, Frank's insistence on thematic totality makes it closer kin to *Cane* than the alienated social landscape of *Winesburg*.

City Block's narrative system reflects Frank's embrace of unanimisme, and thereby indicates Bourne's critical role in modern network aesthetics. Frank was a friend of Romains, and his interest in the French poet and essayist was widely known among the American literati.[7] His understanding of Romains's work was shaped by Bourne's reading of unanimisme, which, as chapter 1 has shown, placed a heavy emphasis on Bourne's understandings of "group-life" and the Beloved Community. Although Romains's focus was the interactions between individuals and technology in the urban milieu, Bourne and Frank abstracted unanimisme to deal with the individual's relation to a coherent social space. In *City Block*, unanimisme is channeled by Benati, the 15-year-old whose story concludes the cycle, and whose psychic visions organize the preceding stories. Benati's psychic consciousness facilitates the

Block's unanimisme, leading him to recognize the "group-life" of the various individuals living there. Scruggs and VanDemarr put it this way: "Frank saw the whole of his short-story cycle as depicting the invisible unity and spirit of the characters within the city block rather than the isolation and separateness of the characters in *Winesburg*; the development of *City Block* was the revelation of an invisible unity, not the growth of an individual experience like that experienced by Anderson's George Willard" (117–18).

The adoption of unanimisme in *Cane* may seem counterintuitive, given that unanimisme was so rooted in the urban experience for Romains and that the settings in *Cane* are predominantly rural—or that Bourne's adoption of Romains is so blind to the matters of race that preoccupy Toomer's texts. Nonetheless, the spirit of unanimisme guides Toomer's work. It was during the summer of 1922 when Toomer read *City Block*, and the experience radically altered his conception of *Cane*, which up to that point he had been thinking of as a collection of pieces without any integrative force (119). Generalized beyond the narrow confines of Romains's theory, Frank's introduction of unanimisme allowed Toomer to link past and present, self and other, urban and rural, white and black into the networks comprising *Cane*. Unanimisme provided the fundamental logic by which Toomer began to see the assorted texts of *Cane* emerging as a network.

Sugarcane, the agrarian corollary to the technology of Romains's urban milieu, is critical to the "group-life" that is asserted across the array of forms and characters in *Cane*. This work begins to register already on the title page, in a verse epigraph: "Oracular. / Redolent of fermenting syrup, / Purple of the dusk, / Deep-rooted cane" (*Cane* iii). A close reading of these lines reveals that cane is not only a material device linking the text's fragments but also a figuration of tradition that in turn connects generations from the antebellum period to Toomer's present. The cane is "oracular" not because it carries any prophetic or predictive qualities but because it speaks—establishing the trope of vocalizing cane that recurs throughout "Kabnis"—and therefore can testify to the passage of history. That it is "deep-rooted" suggests that cane is both embedded in the soil and in African American history itself through the toil of slavery and sharecropping as well as circulating as a commodity vital to the founding of the nation. Cane, then, performs two networking functions: it is the ligament connecting forms, characters, and places in the text; it also draws relational lines across African American generations. Thus the "group-life" of

Toomer's unanimisme at once inscribes the interconnections that constitute a "group-life" of the text and at the same time enacts the connections of the "group-life" that is group identity. With this double signification of cane in mind, I turn to the politics of *Cane*'s networks of form and content.

Allegories of a Distributed Americanism

Shortly after publishing *Cane*, Toomer rather famously began denying racial identification in terms of black and white and instead took to identifying his race as "American." This desire to "Americanize" generically and to strip racial affiliation from his identity and from his works manifests in the essays and autobiographical writings that followed *Cane*. As Scruggs and VanDemarr have shown, Toomer's post-*Cane* writings mark a shaky historical record that is bent on biographical revision and self-fashioning.[8] His revisionism is particularly evident in the suppression of his leftist leanings in the late 1910s and early 1920s, they argue, and also in his muting of the racial politics he was engaged in while writing *Cane* (83). Following Toomer's own self-fashioning, some readings of *Cane* try to locate that refusal of racial politics in the text. This window of racial identification, which Scruggs and VanDemarr say was cresting between 1919 and 1922, enables us, however, to read *Cane* as invested in group identity—a "group-life" at the heart of unanimisme. *Cane*'s distributed form and content, paired with Toomer's investment in group identity, demands a fundamental reconsideration of the author's race politics and his vision of the nation. Toomer's experiments with networks of form and content indicate the network's central role in the aesthetics of American modernism, and demonstrate how American moderns were beginning to rely on the network as a conceptual tool to rethink their changing milieu—and in Toomer's case, the dynamics of race in America.

Several recent studies of *Cane* have characterized the work's formulations of race as built around hybridity and biracialism. In large part, these readings comport with Toomer's post-*Cane* "American" racial identification, and they draw their conclusions about the politics of the text accordingly. Rudolph P. Byrd and Henry Louis Gates Jr., for example, write that Toomer's radical racial identification makes him "a pioneering theorist of hybridity" and suggest that, perhaps influenced by the Mexican writer and activist Jose Vasconcelos, Toomer evoked the mixed-race figure based on the positive associations of hybridity, rejecting any sense of racial purity and instead locating *mestizaje* as a utopian future for mankind (xxxviii–xxxix). Similarly, Joel B. Peckham nods to textual hybridity when he writes that the disparate elements of the text expose "false dichotomies and separations that are both literary and social" (275). Mark Whalan argues that *Cane* adopts hybridrity in structure as well as theme. Following George Hutchinson's pronouncement of Toomer's work as a "biracial text" (Whalan 216), such efforts again demonstrate the difficulty scholars have met with treating *Cane*'s formal complexities and for interpreting their ramifications for the text's social critiques. Moreover, in their figurations of hybridity and fusion, this scholarship also represents one side of the powerful dialectical tension of modernism—the pull toward homogenization—typifying the period and against which Toomer was writing.

Arguments for *Cane*'s textual fusion, however, simply are not supported by the text's collagelike formal organization. Karen Jackson Ford, in a study asserting the importance of poetry in *Cane*, argues against the hybridity of the text: "notwithstanding excellent recent scholarship on *Cane* that explores its efforts to break out of the fiercely inadequate binarisms of American racial discourse. . . . *Cane*'s generic multiplicity amounts not to formal hybridity but to formal essentialism" (17). The formal politics of *Cane* certainly does reject traditional binaries of American discourses on race—not with a hybrid refusal of binaries but with a constellar model that widens the field of discussion. Accordingly, we should replace the figuration of hybridity with that of the network to understand Toomer's use of network aesthetics to theorize race.

Cane's distributed formulations undertake a new model of racial and ethnic interdependence. In doing so, the text poses a significant critique of two of the prevailing discourses of race and ethnicity in the years leading up to its publication—the same conditions to which Bourne responded with his thesis of a distributed national identity in "Trans-National America" (1916). On the one hand, the nation was tilting toward an increasingly atomized treatment of racial and ethnic difference, as emergent discourses of cultural pluralism demonstrate. On the other hand, the melting pot remained attractive for many as a figure of national fusion, with figures such as Theodore Roosevelt advocating "100 Percent Americanism" during the preparedness campaigns. Xenophobic and nationalist sentiment hardened during the Great War, with the nativist strand of Americanism climaxing in the 1920s and resulting in the 1924 National Origins Act. More directly related to the content of *Cane*, this very same Americanism was exhibited first and foremost by the Ku Klux Klan, which was surging in the early 1920s.[9] This is certainly not the Americanism Toomer had in mind when he pronounced his race "American," but the tension between the two treatments of racial difference—homogeneity and dispersal, the key cultural logic of modernism in this case mapped onto one of the period's prominent social tensions—is important in situating the politics of *Cane*'s formal experiments. In this context, *Cane*'s networks perform an important mediation of the period's prevailing discourses of race, providing an alternative rendering of social organization. In the process of this mediation, Toomer challenges for the terrain of "Americanism," which was then being contested by reactionary movements.

Responding to these contexts, the text's formal networks intervene in *Cane*'s conception of race and nation, enabling a nuanced vision of American race relations that operates at two levels. First, if we read *Cane*'s "generic multiplicity" as an allegory of race, then the network becomes a figure for all of the United States' racial and ethnic diversity. This reading is staked more on the allegorical level of form than on the level of plot and character, though we can still see such racial interdependence in the story of Becky, "the white woman who had two Negro sons" and who, though exiled by both white and black communities, is clandestinely supported by them—to name just one example of a localized reading of racial interdependence in the text. Drawing from the text's formal schemes of interdependence, a networked configuration of races offers many significant reconceptualizations of the possibilities for American culture. A model of decentralization, the network disperses whites' hegemonic power across the racial spectrum of the nation—or at the very least dilutes its concentration. Toomer's allegory of form does not change the reality of juridical or economic inequalities of the races, especially because Jim Crow remained widespread and insuperable, but it does offer a utopian model to strive toward, perhaps as a truly distributed corrective to the "separate but equal" standards. Indeed, Toomer's adoption of network aesthetics shares this utopian note with Bourne's transnationalism thesis.

This model radically challenges the mode of interaction between the races, especially compared to the hybridity model to which many contemporary readers of *Cane* subscribe. Instead of the hybridity model's dubious analogue of racial fusion, the network offers a model of interdependence. This model raises the question of essentialism, perhaps, but its virtue lies in its ability to allow for the tradition of group identity while still demanding the cooperation of discrete racial and ethnic traditions in the "group-life" of the nation. Such a model of interconnection and interdependence makes the network an attractive figure through which *Cane* can resolve the many cultural and racial tensions it represents—and especially the abundance of those tensions in the Jim Crow South.

The Martinique essayist, poet, novelist, and dramaturge Edouard Glissant illuminates *Cane*'s allegorical work in his theories of *antillanité* and Relation. For Glissant, antillanité, or Caribbeanness, is not a fixed state of identity, nor is it confined to identity in its application. Instead, Caribbeanness is a state of relationality—one that emerges in the postcolonial situation but that still ranges out to apply to all features of life under globalization.[10] Contrasting Caribbeanness with the hybridity of creoleness, he situates antillanité alongside Deleuze and Guattari's rhizome: "The notion of the rhizome maintains, therefore, the idea of rootedness but challenges that of a totalitarian root. Rhizomatic thought is the principle behind what I call the Poetics of Relation, in which each and every identity is extended through a relationship with the Other" (*Poetics* 11). Indeed, Glissant's relationality, which J. Michael Dash describes as a system of "archipelagos of culture," reads like Bourne's "Trans-National America," only having been shorn of its Eurocentrism to recognize its full distributive capacity (23). Rooted in conditions of the postcolonial Caribbean, Glissant's thesis is, like Bourne's, an amalgam of lived experience and utopian horizon.

Favoring distribution over hybridity, the relationality of antillanité plots a line of continuity from Toomer's distribution of race relations into deconstructive, postcolonial thought, and perhaps relieves *Cane* of the charge of essentialism by distinguishing "root" from "relational" identities. More significantly, however, Glissant's work also marks a counterpoint to the allegorical work of *Cane*. Toomer's utopian impulse takes place—perhaps *must* take place—at an allegorical remove. Allegory in this case may reflect the period's very real pressures on who was allowed to speak and what imaginaries were allowed to be spoken. More likely, allegory underscores the insurmountable task of Toomer's distributed schema—as if it were a utopian wish fulfillment that by its very nature remains perpetually incomplete. But this feature of network aesthetics would begin to diminish as Bourne's influence on subsequent moderns became less and less direct. Indeed, the following chapters demonstrate that although distribution carries a utopian charge in Bourne's and Toomer's work, it takes on more variable applications for subsequent writers, often doing without allegory to address other crises of the period.

Although this utopian charge defines my reading of early network aesthetics, recent scholarship has been less sanguine about the politics of networks. For example, Alexander R. Galloway and Eugene Thacker dispute the utopian politics of networks, observing its organization of both the United States military and Al Qaeda and concluding the form has no inherent politics—reactionary, progressive, or otherwise. Yet Galloway and Thacker do concede that a celebration of distributed networks may have been more appropriate earlier in the twentieth century. Is not Jim Crow such a moment calling for the relational and rhizomatic, with its rigid binaries and its patently false claims to distribution—"separate but equal"? For *Cane*, the allegory of a networked social space is radical indeed in its critique of hierarchical binaries.

Toomer's second intervention into network aesthetics lies in the relation of the individual to the whole. *Cane*'s theorization of race honors Toomer's ostensibly contradictory investments in individualism and group identity. Whalan characterizes Toomer's letters as demonstrating a commitment "to individualism as inherent to an archetypally American identity" (4)—an apt description of Toomer, who so often chafed at group classifications and spurned social affiliation. But that impulse, set alongside his intense interest in race politics during the writing of *Cane*, creates a node-network relationship that is the basic structure of the text itself. As with its figural resolution of racial and cultural conflicts, the network offers a model to preserve individuality while recognizing the collective project of the "group-life." Toomer's use of the network as a model for conceiving of the nation and its culture and of the individual's relation to both again demonstrates his debt to Frank and, through Frank, demonstrates the influence of Bourne and the cadre of Young America thinkers. Casey Nelson Blake characterizes their project as "a communitarian vision of self-realization through participation in a democratic culture" (2)—a large part of which, I argue, relied on networked figurations. Bourne's "Trans-National America" situated the nation as a distributed "federation of cultures" that would allow the United States to become a "cosmopolitan federation of national colonies, of foreign cultures, from whom the sting of devastating competition has been removed" (115, 117). Frank borrowed the networked dynamics of unanimisme as the model for *City Block* and also drew on the figure in *Our America* to illustrate the entanglement of the United States' cultural constituencies, offering an equal claim to "American culture" for Puritan New England, the American Southwest, industrial Chicago, and so on. Bourne's response to prewar ruptures in national identity tightly corresponds to Toomer's renovated "Americanism," as both recognize the network's potential to move a nation in crisis toward a utopian plane. With Frank and especially Bourne as forebears, it is not surprising that Toomer would deploy a networked figuration to rethink the race relations of the nation. Although his use of such models is more intuitive than Bourne's and Frank's overtly political formations, the model itself is invested with a highly political, even utopian charge in its organization of national space.

That *Cane* sets about reorganizing the nation with such a wide array of connective devices—in both the text's form and content—demonstrates how American modernists experimented with networked models to mediate the dialectical tensions of homogeneity and dispersal, using them to reimagine some of the most foundational conditions of the nation's social organization. Its particular amalgam of network aesthetics, taken alongside Bourne's and Frank's adoptions of unanimisme in pursuit of a "democratic culture," marks but one facet of the moderns' attraction to distributed configurations. Nevertheless, the diverse range of devices used in *Cane* shows in relief the truncation of network aesthetics in contemporary narrative, which emphasizes either the six-degrees-of-separation theory, as David Bordwell would have it, or hyperlinked writing environments, as David Ciccoricco does. Bordwell's framework, for example, would limit *Cane*'s networks only to those ties involving King Barlo, Old David Georgia, and the anonymous draughtsman of the Madonna in the first section of the text, and would fail to recognize Toomer's formal networking schemes. Only with this spatial reading of form does the full dimension of Toomer's network aesthetics come to the fore, enabling readers to see *Cane*'s negotiation of a homogeneous Americanism and an atomized model of identitarianism.

Alongside Bourne's transnationalism thesis, *Cane*'s production of a liberatory, distributed mode of Americanism, fashioned between a homogenizing assimilation and an outright dispersal of racial and ethnic identities, shows modern network aesthetics at its most politically engaged. Anita Loos's *Gentlemen Prefer Blondes* (1925), as the following chapter will detail, maintains this liberatory note while backing away from Toomer's polemicism. The strength of *Cane*'s political critique is particularly evident in Toomer's dual deployments of networks, as the allegory of *Cane*'s form works alongside the content of community built around commodity circulation to establish a flattened, decentralized model of social organization. The text's modes of networking demonstrates the distinctly modernist entanglement of politics and form—indeed, demonstrates the politics *of* form—as *Cane*'s formal strategies to negotiate the tendencies toward totalization and dispersal act not only as an aesthetic principle but as a theory of the nation. Accordingly, *Cane* establishes the network as a signal device of modernist aesthetics and theory and invites readers to consider how such social formations might be practiced.

3

Public Spaces and Distributed Settings in Anita Loos's *Gentlemen Prefer Blondes*

One night shortly after the attack on Pearl Harbor, Anita Loos received a knock on the door. She was expecting guests for dinner but instead found a young man informing her that her house was being requisitioned as a checkpoint in the civil defense of California's coastline. The two men who would be stationed outside with communications equipment soon became part of her thriving social life. In her diaries she recalls one evening when she gave a party and invited the volunteers inside. When the young men finally agreed, they were thrilled to see the bombshell stars Marie Wilson and Frances Rafferty and remarked that their friends would never believe their story. "Call them up and ask them over," Loos insisted (Carey 202). Her biographer Gary Carey writes that "the regiment arrived and soon everyone, including Anita, was jitterbugging" (202). "The best party I ever gave," Loos would recall (202). Such occasions would be routine for the volunteers who cycled through this checkpoint. Beyond Wilson and Rafferty, it is unclear whom they would have met there, but with Loos's diverse social sets the possibilities for meeting celebrities and literati were vast. During this period she was crocheting socks, sweaters, and "peter heaters" for the enlisted men with Paulette Goddard—her husband, Charlie Chaplin, however, was a longshot, as he and Goddard were separating. She kept company with Katherine Hepburn, Greta Garbo, and Joan Crawford. And Loos herself was no small catch in this regard: as a screenwriter in the late 1910s, she received as much coverage in the celebrity press as Mary Pickford and Lillian Gish, and each crest of her career would be punctuated by a renewed interest from the fan magazines (50). Loos was equally likely to entertain the men with literati such as Aldous Huxley or, if he were visiting from the East Coast, H. L. Mencken. Whoever the guests turned out to be, the young men were lucky indeed to have been assigned to what she referred to as "Fort Loos."

Her informal service at Fort Loos, along with her dedicated tending of a victory garden throughout World War II, marks a quiet social conservatism that may seem at odds with her most famous character, the scandalous flapper Lorelei Lee of *Gentlemen Prefer Blondes* (1925). But Fort Loos is also a token of Loos's spatial reorganization of class and gender norms. Fort Loos posed not a fixed cross-section of American class stratification. Rather, in making dance partners of civil volunteers, movie stars, and untold others, Loos asserted a distributed understanding of social space. It is a project that typifies *Blondes*'s hotel and cocktail party settings.

Loos provides a unique study of such network aesthetics as they appear in popular modernisms, in large part because she was equally comfortable among Hollywood stars and the intelligentsia. Loos got her big break writing title cards for D. W. Griffith's *Intolerance* (1916), and proceeded to notch 152 screen credits with long stretches writing for Douglas Fairbanks and Clark Gable. Carey writes that unlike many of her modernist peers she did not look down on screenwriting and even "enjoyed writing for star personalities" such as Crawford (150). With *Blondes* she turned to popular fiction. After being serialized in *Harper's Bazar* in 1925, it rang in second among the best-selling novels in the United States in 1926 (Churchwell 158). The novella's sales led to extensive franchising,[1] and Loos's flapper resurfaced with some frequency for another sixty years: in short pieces for periodicals such as *New York Times Magazine* and *Town and Country* from 1927 to 1984; in a short-lived *Blondes* play in 1926; in a 1928 film adaptation that is now lost; in a musical starring Carol Channing that began a 90-week run in 1949; and most famously in Howard Hawks's 1953 film starring Marilyn Monroe and Jane Russell. At the same time, however, *Blondes* also demonstrates an affinity for high modernism, reflected in part by the letters of appreciation Loos received from James Joyce, William Faulkner, Aldous Huxley, and Edith Wharton—some of which, such as Huxley's, might better be described as mash notes.[2] The text gestures toward high modernism in its narrational devices and sexual politics, and above all in its ambivalence toward the apparatus of mass culture, particularly Hollywood, in which Loos herself was ensconced.

The relatively scant scholarship on *Blondes* tends to focus on feminist criticism, and with good reason. In dealing with sexuality and gendered work and anchoring itself around two remarkably independent women, the text demands discussions of gender and sexuality. To complement that tradition of criticism, this chapter explores *Blondes*'s settings, which are often public spaces that undermine the hierarchies of social class and the gendered norms of public and private spheres. In other words, while the adjacent chapters study the formal experiments of Jean Toomer's *Cane* (1923) and John Dos Passos's *U.S.A.* trilogy (1930–36), this chapter locates setting as a major field of the moderns' engagements with network aesthetics. It would be easy enough to see Lorelei Lee as a sort of Frankenstein's monster unleashed on the Social Register elite, as Regina Barreca suggests in her introduction to the 1998 edition of the text. But drawing on the uniquely modern experience of the public through the setting of hotels, Lorelei achieves a networked mode of social organization, paradoxically ascending class ranks at the same time that she flattens them into distribution. Situated between two polarities of social organization—a massified culture suggested in Loos's and Lorelei's Hollywood careers and the divisions of social classes that were ossifying throughout the 1920s—*Blondes* asserts a networked model of community to mediate class stratification and the gendering of public and private. Accordingly, *Blondes* brings the popular to bear on the cultural logic of modernism.

All the World's a Ritz

Written in the form of Lorelei's diary, *Blondes* foregrounds the sly manipulations of the aspiring authoress as she angles for material gain, leaving readers to guess at what she may trade for it. According to Lorelei, "kissing your hand may make you feel very very good but a diamond and safire bracelet lasts forever" (55). Her clear-eyed, parodic depiction of traditional marital contract relations—the exchange of sex for material security—is at the center of all of Lorelei's relationships and much of her conflict with Dorothy, whose primary interest in men, Lorelei suspects, places too little emphasis on their pocketbooks. As Barreca notes, "Lorelei transforms those elements most feared by most women of her day—independence, sexual attractiveness, male attention, a life uncluttered by family ties—into what she desires; in other words, she turns everything that could possibly intimidate her into something that will aid her" (xviii). In this light, Lorelei's defining characteristic is her refusal to be confined to private domestic roles, and her adventures in the public sphere celebrate an independence many women of the period would find simultaneously enviable and daunting.

But Lorelei and Dorothy are not content to disrupt only conventional sexuality and the traditional gender roles of heterosexual relationships. They are also intent on unsettling and even reorganizing social class. The upheaval of social class is in part evident in the plot's narrative of social ascension: in Lorelei's repeatedly stated goal of entering the lofty ranks of the Social Register, her pervasive anxiety over middle-class strategies of improvement, and her calculated accumulation of material capital, as well as in Dorothy's pursuit of cultural capital—in sum, what Barreca refers to as "the socially disruptive nature of Loos's characters" (xiv). But an equally important part of *Blondes*'s disruption of the class system is predicated on the same rejection of the public/private binary identified by feminist criticism. By taking advantage of the public spaces of hotels, Lorelei and Dorothy create contact zones where service workers, the refined elite, and working- and middle-class people intermingle. These contact zones are more than comic devices that display Loos's wit and humor by lampooning the tensions that arise when classes intersect. Instead, these settings stage the distribution of class strata and mark a paradox between their flattening of social class and Lorelei's ambition of class ascension.

For Lorelei, this contact setting is primarily associated with the Ritz, which is her standard of the prestige and wealth to which she aspires at the same time that it facilitates the flattening of class strata. The Ritz is a common setting for Lorelei's exploits in the United States and throughout her Grand Tour, and it is central to her understanding of class and gender norms. Lorelei establishes the Ritz's centrality to *Blondes* in the text's very first sentence, a casual reference to assert her social advancement: "A gentlemen friend and I were dining at the Ritz last evening and he said that if I took a pencil and a paper and put down all of my thoughts it would make a book" (3). In addition to its generic marker of wealth, the Ritz also held a special allure during the modern period. Turn-of-the-century art critic Bernard Berenson coined the term "Ritzonia" in reference to the famously luxurious chain of hotels, and the term captures the allure that the Ritz franchise had during the 1920s, standing for many—especially writers such as Fitzgerald and Hemingway, who fawned over the bar at Paris's Ritz during their days on the Left Bank—as the epitome of high living during the carefree Roaring Twenties (Montgomery-Massingberd 147, 153). Loos's use of the Ritz, however, was more than a topical marker of the decade's excesses. Lorelei's constant invocation of the Ritz draws on the distinctly democratized formation of the hotel that dates back to the earliest days of the republic, and especially on the powerful iconography of the grand hotel—also referred to as the palace or imperial hotel—that dates back to the Gilded Age.

It is easy to forget, given the atomizing nature of the motor hotel and the faster paces of business travel and tourism that prevail today, that until the middle of the twentieth century the hotel was considered first and foremost a public space—even in the case of decadent, elite institutions such as the Ritz franchises. In *The American Scene* (1907), his account of returning to the United States after some twenty-five years of living in England, Henry James attests to the hotel's critical function in modern American life, writing that "the present is more and more the day of the hotel" (73). Although James seems genuinely surprised that provincial Americans were beginning to produce a civilization to rival Europe's through the opulent Waldorf-Astoria and other grand hotels, other moderns understood the hotel not as an inheritance from Europe but, given the democratic character of its public spaces, as a uniquely American institution. Jefferson Williamson's *The American Hotel* (1930) celebrates this tradition and argues that unlike European lodgings that had once been exclusively the domain of the elite, American hotels "were built for equalitarian enjoyment" given that the public could enjoy hotels' lobbies and bars gratis (9). The hotel, according to Williamson, was the undisputed center of social life because it hosted all of the community's formal events, making it the center of political, business, and most other social activity. "Democracy's leaven," he calls it (9). Williamson's tone often betrays a note of American exceptionalism, and at times his review verges on the jeremiad, suggesting the closure of these public spaces that would ultimately arrive in the mid-century hotel's increased emphasis on privacy and personalized service and the breaking up of the hotel's interior spaces.

We can see in Williamson's description some continuity with the hotel of today, which still hosts professional meetings such as the MLA convention, political rallies, wedding receptions, and so on. For the purposes of this chapter, however, the discontinuities between Williamson's hotels and ours are noteworthy. Through the middle of the last century, the hotel's public spaces—its bars and lobbies, its restaurants and parlors, its reading rooms—provided its community with informal settings of social exchange every day, in addition to hosting major events. The social center for travelers and locals alike, the hotel acted as a contact zone along two planes, putting individuals into contact with each other and putting a community into contact with the nation. In his seminal study *Hotel* (2007), A. K. Sandoval-Strausz writes that this role in facilitating contact was the primary identity of hotels through the modern period, even more than the accommodations of their private guest rooms.[3] The dining rooms epitomized the hotel's investment in egalitarian, heterogeneous sociability—so much so that one journalist referred to them as "the tangible republic" (Williamson 210). This social exchange was in large part predicated on the American plan, the meal plan that prevailed in American hotels through the Great War. It consisted of four heaping meals throughout the day, provided at a flat rate included in the cost of the room and served on long tables that spanned the length of the dining room. Although Sandoval-Strausz concedes that this free-for-all arrangement "was hardly conducive to good table manners," he positions it as central to the hotel's construction of public space because it demanded contact between strangers at the table (169).

Lodging at a hotel or partaking of its American plan was a mostly exclusive affair restricted by cost and racial segregation, but participating in its public spaces was not—a key to the hotel's claim for democratized ideals, and a history that Loos draws on for Lorelei's reorganization of social hierarchy. Lobbies, lounges, and parlors were consistently full of nonresidents; small exhibitions were held to increase foot traffic inside the hotel, and drinks at the bar and meals in the dining hall were priced to a wide base of patrons.[4] At James's revered Waldorf-Astoria, Lorelei's Ritzes, or working- or middle-class accommodations, any reasonably dressed white person could make use of the hotel's public spaces. The hotel's public function was so commonly assumed that it would become a central feature of the 1964 Civil Rights Act. Because these spaces facilitated exchanges from individuals of a variety of backgrounds and created a democratized, if exclusively white, social heterogeneity, Sandoval-Strausz appraises the hotel's contact zone as a facilitator of modern cosmopolitanism, as it created a "multiplier effect" of myriad contacts between locals and travelers.[5] There is a latent tension between homogeneity and dispersal—suggestive of a monolithic class apparatus in the exclusivity of its lodgings and conversely of a fragmented social body in its array of private rooms—that the hotel negotiates in the distributive functions of its public spaces. In other words, the hotel was a key setting in which Americans lived the cultural logic of modernism.

For *Blondes,* the hotel's distributive force emerges in Lorelei's and Dorothy's knowable relationships with workers. These bonds constitute a major part of their experiences within hotels and lay the groundwork for their rejection of the grand hotel's class stratification. Although the public spaces of the hotel are designed for the meeting and mixing of patrons, a surprising number of the contacts Lorelei and Dorothy make in their Ritz-hopping adventures involve hotel service workers. In London, a bellhop named Harry is an integral part of Lorelei's ruse to ensnare the aristocrat Sir Francis Beekman. Lorelei describes him as a friend "who is quite a nice boy who is called Harry and who we talk to quite a lot" (44). She relies on him to execute the plan to corner Beekman into claiming credit for sending orchids to Lorelei's room—flowers that Lorelei paid for herself in a ploy to loosen up Beekman's wallet with the ultimate goal of attaining a $7,500 diamond tiara (44). In Paris, Leon, a "waiter friend" whom they meet at the Ritz restaurant, serves as a confidant. He translates the dialogue between "Robber" and "Louie"—Lorelei's malapropistic transliteration of the names of two detectives hired by Beekman's wife to recover the ill-gotten tiara—so that Lorelei can counter their ruse with one of her own. They return to this strategy in the 1928 sequel, *But Gentlemen Marry Brunettes,* in which Lorelei and Dorothy cozy up to Tony, a waiter at the Algonquin Hotel restaurant, to discuss "ideas" and later to make connections with the literati of the Algonquin Round-Table (139). Their ties to Harry and Leon are reflected in the numerous contacts the duo makes with workers outside hotels. For example, Lorelei's relationship with her maid Lulu is so close that she entrusts her with the all-important task of "education" and "improving her mind": "I told Lulu to let all of the house work go and spend the day reading a book entitled 'Lord Jim' and then tell me about it, so that I would improve my mind while Gerry is away" (*Blondes* 13). At almost every stage of the novel, Lorelei and Dorothy have strong ties to the people who work to sustain their comfortable lifestyles, and these ties are often established in hotel settings.

To observe these relationships is not to imply that Lorelei and Dorothy are sympathetic with labor interests. In each case, a relationship with a worker is the means to an end: Harry is a role player in the orchids ruse, Leon is necessary for deciphering "the French landguage," Tony is useful in cozying up to the Algonquin's literary scene, and Lulu tends to the household. But this is the case with all of Lorelei's relationships, regardless of class, as each of her suitors serves as an instrument in her pursuit of material gain. These relationships are as sincere as any form of human interaction Lorelei knows. She refers to these workers as friends, and she and Dorothy relate to them earnestly and without any condescension marking their class difference.

Such free exchanges with workers reflect the class anxieties that pervade *Blondes*. Lorelei's fixation on "education" and "improvement" signals a middle-class sensibility that is a common subject in criticism of the text. Mark McGurl explains that in addition to Lorelei's quest for material accumulation, she pursues the immaterial values of middle-class virtue: "Her tale is also conspicuously, if satirically, about the acquisition of culture, an aesthetic education Lorelei refers to as 'improving her mind'" (106). These middle-class keywords often act as code for the carefully avoided sexual economy that permeates Lorelei's diary. For example, she writes that "when a gentleman is interested in educating a girl, he likes to stay and talk about the topics of the day until quite late, so I am quite fatigued the next day" (4). Similarly, of one suitor's rivalry she remarks: "Mr. Spoffard might not seem to understand why Mr. Eisman seems to spend quite a lot of money to get me educated" (87).

Loos's selection of Little Rock, Arkansas as Lorelei's birthplace also marks these class tensions: it sits right in the middle of the region that Mencken dubbed "the Sahara of the Bozart" in 1920. Carey describes Loos as "a confirmed Menckenite" (86), and in situating Lorelei's origin in Little Rock she adopts his antagonism toward the South. In the introduction to the twenty-second edition of *Blondes*, published in 1963, Loos writes that "I wanted Lorelei to be a symbol of the lowest possible mentality of our nation" and therefore "chose Little Rock for my heroine's early years" ("Biography of a Book" 55). Still later, she would say Mencken had a more direct hand in crafting Lorelei's background: "It was at a cocktail party that Menck gave me the idea of choosing Little Rock as the proper birthplace for the idiotic blonde whose story I was writing" ("Cocktail Parties" 95–96). But as Loos was well aware, Mencken's "Sahara" of intellectual and cultural life suggested the cultural anxieties of class much more than it questioned regional intellectual capacities. "The poor white trash are now in the saddle," Mencken wrote of one case study of Southern intellectual-cultural decline (186). These class anxieties loom large in *Blondes*.

Lorelei is self-conscious of her class position, as her investment in such middle-class methods of social ascension as "education" and "improvement" demonstrates. She even attempts an outright revision of her own narrative in order to bolster her class status. When reporters covering her engagement to

Henry Spoffard, the Reform advocate from an established Philadelphia family, ask about what she did before becoming engaged, she tells them: "I was nothing but a society girl from Little Rock" (*Blondes* 100). This is a laughable claim, readers know, because Lorelei has an unmistakably working-class origin story: she worked as a stenographer in Little Rock, but her secretarial position came to an abrupt end when her boss found himself shot by her revolver. "It seems that I had a revolver in my hand and it seems that the revolver had shot Mr. Jennings," Lorelei recalls (25). This revision is important as a bid to consolidate Lorelei's engagement to Spoffard, positioning herself as socially equal to his WASPy family. But it also fits the broader narrative of ascension, in which her patronage of grand hotels is key to the realization of her aspirations. Not only does the Ritz offer the spectacle of wealth befitting the class status she desires, but it also affords her opportunities to mix with the elite in the hotel's public spaces.

Although hotels offer Lorelei a chance to mix with service employees behind the scenes, they also offer her an opportunity to broadcast her status by ostentatious displays of connections to the elite and celebrities. In the restaurant of the London Ritz, Lorelei and Dorothy spot the famed vaudeville and silent film actress Fanny Ward and hastily attach to her: "We asked her to come over to our table and we were all three delighted to see each other. Because I and Fanny have known each other for about five years" (34–35). The three of them get on so well that they go shopping together, and Fanny teaches Lorelei some of her fashion tricks. At the bar in the Paris Ritz, Lorelei and Dorothy again bid for status by attaching themselves to celebrities such as the Dolly sisters and Pearl White. Lorelei recalls that the first time she saw her future husband was at the New York Ritz when he scorned the scandalous actress Peggy Hopkins Joyce out of his Reformist "Prespyterian" convictions. And when she finally breaks things off with Mr. Eisman, secure in her relational exchange with Spoffard, she softens the blow by offering herself as social capital for him: "I told him that he really ought to be very proud of me, because in the future, when he would see me at luncheon at the Ritz as the wife of the famous Henry H. Spoffard, I would always bow to him, if I saw him, and he could point me out to all of his friends and tell them that it was he, Gus Eisman himself, who educated me up to my station" (121). In the short span of the novella, the Ritz's public spaces stage a revolution: Lorelei initially uses them to glean status and prestige from celebrities and the elite with whom she brushes elbows, and ultimately she uses them to bestow her own social capital onto Eisman and others who could claim gainful connections to her.

In this sense, Lorelei's use of the hotel's contact zones is rather mundane. She creates networks of social capital by forging and highlighting connections to the rich and famous. But when this behavior is paired with her affiliation with the service workers who help sustain these luxurious hotels, *Blondes* rings an unexpected note in its own narrative of upward mobility: Lorelei's navigation of these public spaces signals a paradox of ascension and flattening. On the one hand, she uses these spaces to parade her own material and cultural accumulation and display her connections to the Social Register elite—and her very presence there completes her rise from her lowly roots in "Saharan" Arkansas. On the other hand, Lorelei persistently cultivates connections to the hotel staff as if she were still maintaining connections with her working-class history, and without a thought for the scorn the WASP elite would have for such conduct. In both cases, she carefully develops social networks—a leisurely set to burnish her credentials of social capital, and a working set to help her establish and maintain those credentials. Situated between these two classed networks, Lorelei acts as a pivotal nodal exchange, bridging the nodal exchanges between the elite and workers, simultaneously rising up the ranks of class hierarchy and flattening them with her ambivalent affiliations.

This distributive logic is so engrained in the text that Lorelei is held up for ridicule for seeming not to understand its gravity. In the text's final diary entry, Lorelei recalls meeting Mr. Eisman for lunch at the Ritz to inform him of her engagement to Spoffard, presumably relying on the public nature of the spot to defray any outburst pursuant to the news. After offering herself as social capital to offset any hurt feelings, her last thoughts on Mr. Eisman show a comic misrecognition of the same social distribution that she relies on throughout the text: "I really do not care what he says to his friends, because, after all, his friends are not in my set, and whatever he says to them will not get around in my circle" (121). Loos's readers know better by now. The logic of the text dictates that Lorelei's tie to Mr. Eisman will never be fully severed. Their tie may weaken, but they will remain entangled in the same networked field. Loos takes for granted that her readers understand this situation. Making Lorelei the object of the joke only affirms the indispensable role of networks in *Blondes*'s diegesis.

The stuff of this joke has been observed in criticism of *Blondes*, though without reckoning with its networked project. For instance, McGurl characterizes *Blondes* as preoccupied with "the problem of social indistinction and cultural leveling" as it satirizes mechanisms of distinction by imagining a context "where even morons like Lorelei Lee are encouraged to write books and even the Philadelphia social elite try their hand at film scenarios" (109). McGurl's narrative of "indistinction" and "leveling," however, does not fully account for the devices by which it is achieved. For it is not only her undermining of traditional tools and practices of social distinction—her claim for authorial legitimacy, her dubious means of "improving her mind," her continual upbraiding of Dorothy's "unrefined" behavior—that yield a leveling of the social hierarchy that Lorelei intends to climb. Lorelei achieves this flattening by drawing relational lines in all directions, with no regard for class status.

It is equally important to observe that Lorelei conducts these globetrotting adventures in the hotel's public spaces as a single, unchaperoned woman. The hotel provides a space for Lorelei to finesse the gendered boundaries of public life and private domesticity in addition to the stratifications of class. Much of the feminist criticism of *Blondes* is interested in how Lorelei manages to avoid the suffocation of being a "kept" woman—a negotiation that is largely enabled by the public spaces of the hotel.[6] Although Dorothy's putative function on the Grand Tour is to act as proxy chaperone for Eisman, ever desirous of keeping Lorelei under his control, she and Lorelei both make a mockery of Eisman's paternalistic impulses by using his patronage to fund their scandalous exploits. Openly mixing in the hotels, the two enjoy an easy freedom of movement that is a constitutive element of the hotel's public spaces. Their ability to maintain that freedom without conceding their aspirations for social ascension—in other words, to mix freely without tainting themselves with working-class indecorum or, worse, associating themselves with prostitution—would be nearly impossible without the hotel's seal of propriety.

In a way, then, the winking nature of the text comports with a winking nature of the hotel that involves its difficult balance of public and private functions. Loos's sly prose routinely suggests Lorelei's promiscuity. Similarly, just as today the "do not disturb" door hanger retains a special erotic charge, the hotel has connoted scandal from the founding of the institution. Evidence of such conduct is hard to come by for obvious reasons, but Sandoval-Strausz writes that there is a long record of divorces predicated on hotel-related testimony attesting to the hotel's role as a site of illicit affairs, and he notes that prostitution was so closely related to hotels that through the turn of the century upstanding women had to follow strict propriety codes to ensure that they would not be mistaken for sex workers. He writes: "The first word on sex in hotels belongs to a minister who preached that hotels were immoral. Asked why, he replied that any establishment that sold liquor and contained so many beds had to be sinful" (204). The minister's context, of course, predates the Prohibition era of *Blondes* but nonetheless establishes the hotel's iconography in American culture. Lorelei must navigate these propriety codes—public spaces, private rooms, and the risk of private assignations being made public—lest the stigma of sex work impede her goal of social ascension.

Although her activities at the hotel never signal indecency, Lorelei's use of the hotel to disrupt the gendered boundaries of public and private adds another dimension to *Blondes*'s figuration of public spaces. With its public restaurants, lobbies, and bars, along with its private and potentially scandalous chambers, the hotel provides a perfect field for Lorelei to exert herself as an unkept woman and as a social climber. In her pursuit of the wealth, prestige, and power signaled by the grand hotel, Lorelei challenges the public and private norms of gender and inadvertently reorganizes class stratification into a networked field in the hotel's public spaces. This is the true mark of Lorelei's social ambition: she is not, in fact, a social climber but a networker of the social sphere.

The hotel settings stand in counterpoint to another important setting in *Blondes*: Hollywood. Loos's own biography, which would have been known to many readers, accentuates the textual material. Lorelei, readers find in just the second diary entry, was once "doing quite well in the cinema," though readers are to infer that she never advanced far beyond central casting (*Blondes* 6). She conceals this information while courting Spoffard, whose Reform efforts mirror those of John S. Sumner, leader of the New York Society for the Suppression of Vice. Loos is quick to lampoon such Reform work. After splicing out all the controversial frames of a film, Spoffard and his colleagues "put all of the riskay pieces together and they run them over and over again" (102). But Loos saves her most rancorous satire for Hollywood itself. In *Blondes*'s closing act, Lorelei meets Gilbert Montrose, an aspiring scenario writer whose vacuity rivals her own. Montrose is drafting a period piece on Dolly Madison's sex life and holds court with the impressionable flapper: "So according to Mr.

Montrose's opinion Shakespear is a very great playwrite, and he thinks that Hamlet is quite a famous tragedy and as far as novels are concerned he believes that nearly everybody had ought to read Dickens" (113). *Blondes*'s conclusion returns Lorelei to Hollywood, married to Spoffard and partnered with Montrose. The three of them form a symbiotic triangle, with Montrose writing the scripts, Lorelei acting in them, and Spoffard "senshuring" them. "By the time we all got through" with the films, Lorelei writes in her diary, "they would be a work of art" (120). Loos advances a typical high modern aesthete's lament of the culture industry and burlesques her own career as a screenwriter with a satirical inflection of the Hollywood ending.

In the context of *Blondes*'s networked social organization, the invocation of Hollywood's massified culture is inauspicious—and not only as a matter of degraded aesthetics. Rather, Hollywood threatens a homogeneous social organization against the distributive force of Lorelei's hotels. In its massified uniformity, Hollywood ironically aligns with the South, which in Mencken's formulation is culturally and intellectually sterile because its management has been consolidated into a single class stratum. "The vast hemorrhage of the Civil War half exterminated and wholly paralyzed the old aristocracy, and so left the land to the harsh mercies of the poor white trash, now its masters," Mencken laments, but it is unclear whether the problem would be solved were the South's culture to be homogenized under another banner (188). Spoffard marks the dangers of social uniformity in his relationship with Hollywood production and even more patently in his politics. Lorelei observes that he is "100 per cent, of an American" (Loos, *Blondes* 85). Loos's malapropistic invocation of the prewar and interwar discourses of Americanism—an explicit motivator of Randolph Bourne's investment in distributed social space—pairs the specter of nationalist conformity with the homogenizing function of mass culture. In his late modern essay "Masscult and Midcult," Dwight Macdonald draws the connection between these two forms of massification in his observation that people in a mass society live in a state of exhaustion because of an unnatural lack of contact (23). Loos seems to share this lament of the externally organized social body in *Blondes* and in her establishment of Fort Loos. Lorelei's relations are instrumentalized but never abstracted by an external mediator. Setting Hollywood alongside "100 Percent Americanism" and the South in a coalition of totalization, Loos avoids the cliché of the modern's loathing for the popular. Rather, she uses one of the key sites of the popular—the spaces of public heterogeneity—to undermine the massifying potential of the popular in her assertion of distributed social organization. In doing so, Loos joins Bourne and Jean Toomer in a genealogy of networked responses to homogenizing, Americanist discourses.

In addition to its treatment of Hollywood, *Blondes* shows the distinctly modernist quality of network aesthetics in departing from the realist genealogy of hotel representation. In "The Politics of Nonidentity," Ross Posnock reads James's visit to the Waldorf-Astoria in *The American Scene* as part of James's commitment to "nonidentity"—a project that claims its value "by deliberately eluding identification and direct affiliation" (36). In Posnock's reading, James recoils at the hotel's homogenizing function, which epitomizes "modernity's rationalizing, disciplinary imperative" in the management of patrons and in the dissolving of their individual differences into a "'gorgeous golden blur'" (40). Unable to find any affirmation of the unlike at the Waldorf-Astoria, James turns to the Lower East Side in pursuit of nonidentity. This was a common understanding of the hotel shared by other realist projects such as Harold Frederic's *The Damnation of Theron Ware* (1896) or Theodore Dreiser's *Sister Carrie* (1900). *Blondes* signals a break in the understanding of social space and of the hotel particularly. In contrast to the realists' disciplinary monolith, the moderns' hotel distributed the space of its setting and performs a mediation of the cultural logic of modernism. This is true of Loos's Ritz settings, and other modern projects would treat the hotel similarly. For example, *Grand Hotel*, the 1932 film starring Greta Garbo and Joan Crawford, asserts the hotel's distributive force by locating its action in public spaces such as the lobby and the tearoom and by using the switchboard and the revolving door as transitional figures to pass between settings and narrative threads. Architect and theorist Rem Koolhaas ties this distinctly modernist narrative production to the Waldorf-Astoria's opening of a spectacular new venue, having moved north to Park Avenue to free up the lot that would eventually be the site of the Empire State Building:

> In the thirties—when the second Waldorf is being built—the "Hotel" becomes Hollywood's favorite subject. In a sense, it relieves the scriptwriter of the obligation of inventing a plot. A Hotel *is* a plot—a cybernetic universe with its own laws generating random but fortuitous collisions between human beings who would never have met elsewhere. It offers a fertile cross section

through the population, a richly textured interface between social castes, a field for the comedy of clashing manners and a neutral background of routine operations to give every incident dramatic relief. (149–50)

To put it in Posnock's terms, the hotel itself offers nonidentity for the moderns—the very preservation of a heterogeneity that James once had to leave the Waldorf-Astoria in order to find. Whereas the realist could only find difference in discrete settings, the moderns find that difference in the setting of the hotel, where the positions of nonidentity coincide in distribution. For Loos, the hotel was not yet a plot, as it would be for Koolhaas's scriptwriters of the 1930s, but her setting yields the same result: not just a cross-section of classed and gendered experiences but a completely reorganized, distributed social space.

Class, Cocktail Parties, and Networked Space

Although *Blondes* explicitly invokes the homogenizing figures of Hollywood and Americanism, an implicit contrast of dispersal lies in the 1920s contexts of atomizing class discourses. The wealth and ease of the Roaring Twenties, of course, were not universally enjoyed by Americans. The roar's volume and timbre were experienced unevenly across the usual divides of class, race, ethnicity, sex, and gender. As David Goldberg details in *Discontented America*, the depression of 1920–21 hindered the labor movement throughout the so-called Coolidge Prosperity. American business used welfare capitalism as a carrot and open-shop rhetoric as a stick in its antiunion efforts, tying its cause to patriotic fervor under the American Plan of Employment, or simply the "American Plan," as if drawing on the democratic rhetoric of the hotel's meal plan (72). Labor affiliation declined steeply throughout the decade, not to recover until the exigencies of the 1930s. In this climate, income disparity widened and class divisions hardened: shortly after *Blondes*'s publication, roughly thirty percent of the nation's wealth would be held by one percent of the population (88). Poor and unprotected, American workers lived in a constant state of precarity. The homogeneity of mass culture and Americanism, the increasingly rigid divisions of class—these are signal markers of the cultural logic of modernism and the tensions that are mediated in *Blondes*'s networked spaces.

Although Lorelei's use of the hotel's public spaces challenges this class ossification, she is not ignorant of it. In her Grand Tour, the Ritz offers localized spaces of social disruption, and also makes class stratification visible in its networked mapping of wealth—in this case, as a global corollary of the crises in the United States' class system. Throughout her tour, financed by Mr. Eisman to distract her from a rival suitor, the novelist Gerry Lamson, the Ritz marks Lorelei's spatial understanding of the globe: its presence signals a node of power and sophistication, and its absence conversely creates meaning and value in negative space. After stops in London and Paris where the Ritz is the chief attraction, the hotel develops an austere signification. When Lorelei arrives in "the Central of Europe," the leg of the tour that takes her to Munich, Vienna, and finally to Budapest, the Ritz becomes a scarce commodity and in turn signals scarcity. Her hotel in Munich is unnamed, in Vienna she stays at the Bristol Hotel, and the Ritz in Budapest surprises her by redeeming the final stage of her travels: "So we will soon be at the Ritz hotel again and I must say it will be delightful to find a Ritz hotel right in the central of Europe" (*Blondes* 97). Relatively unexplored compared to the other cities she visits, Budapest—"Buda Pest," as she calls it—only offers one attraction, the hotel, that warrants a fleeting mention in Lorelei's travel diary. On this part of her tour, conspicuously organized around the former Central Powers, the relative absence of the Ritz is striking. Instead of the fabulous decadence of a grand hotel, the first sight she observes in Germany is hard labor—a brutal, gendered work that gives Lorelei slight pause to consider her own privilege, or at least to suggest it to readers. Looking out the window of her moving train, she sees something "really quite unusual. Because it was farms, and we saw quite a lot of girls who seemed to be putting small size hay stacks onto large size hay stacks while their husbands seemed to sit at a table under quite a shady tree and drink beer" (75). This scene sets the tone for the remainder of the trip, which Lorelei finds dingy and uncouth. The contrast with the establishing scenes in Ritz hotels in London and Paris informs Lorelei's understanding of class stratification through the geopolitical distributions of wealth in which the reparations-burdened Central Powers occupy negative space and are nearly invisible.

Loos's investment in a radical, if not altogether utopian, social schema to negotiate the tension between this ossified class structure and the massified homogeneity posed by Hollywood may seem at odds with her own social conservatism. In her later years, after her screenwriting career had faded and her days as a novelist were well behind her, Loos turned to writing a set of memoirs and to regular work writing columns and guest pieces for various magazines. Loos's conservatism emerges fully in her nostalgia for the 1920s: nostalgia for romance, which she believes declined with the passing of the twenties; nostalgia for the vitality of the twenties against the perceived sterility of the 1970s and 1980s; nostalgia for the disappearing Renaissance man; nostalgia for the old frontiers of 1920s sexuality, indicated in the snarky and sometimes suspicious tone of her revised catchphrase, "gentlemen prefer gentlemen." In the late 1960s, she even wrote a series of columns for *Family Weekly* giving advice to housewives on such issues as avoiding nervous breakdowns and governing unruly youth—advice that seems well beyond her authority given that Loos scrupulously avoided domestic responsibilities throughout her life and given that her celebrity was largely predicated on her association with the flapper's repudiation of Victorian gender norms.

"Cocktail Parties of the Twenties," an essay from this period that was published in *Gourmet Magazine* in 1970, demonstrates the continuity of Loos's project of reorganizing class relations even into this period of conservatism. And it illuminates another setting of social distribution in *Blondes*, for the cocktail party similarly aspires to a social formation that defies the noncommunity Macdonald ascribes to massification while allowing a heterogeneity akin to Posnock's "nonidentity" genealogy. The essay begins as a celebrity memoir, cataloguing the essential guests for a successful party: F. Scott and Zelda Fitzgerald, H. L. Mencken, George Gershwin, Tallulah Bankhead, and Horace Liveright, as well as a supporting cast of "oodles and oodles of flappers and equal oodles of college men down from Harvard and Yale or up from Princeton" (97). Loos dutifully obliges the reader's interest in celebrity gossip but soon turns to a quasi-sociological study of the role of the requisite bootlegger.

The bootlegger plays an obvious role in supplying the party but is even more important to Loos as a distributor of social space. In her account, any party worth mentioning would handily exhaust the first provisions, requiring the bootlegger to send a confederate for reinforcements—a process that could be repeated indefinitely, bringing more and more of the bootlegging workforce into the party. From this point, the constellar logic of the cocktail party is to assimilate more and more people into its physical and social space. The neighbors inevitably call in a noise complaint, police arrive with an admonition but inexorably find an excuse to stay, and so on. The result would be a flattened grouping of Park Avenue elite, law enforcement, and underworld bootleggers—in other words, a Fort Loos of the East Coast.

This constellar assimilation of different identity positions obtains in several scenes in *Blondes*, as well.[7] Its most prominent expression is in Lorelei's debut party, which Dorothy decides is necessary after Lorelei rewrites herself as "a society girl from Little Rock." The party is another farce, as Lorelei is well past debutante age and her presumed sexual conquests undercut any idea that she is only now entering adulthood. The debut takes place at her apartment over a span of three days and draws on all the ingredients Loos would later suggest for a successful cocktail party: the social elite, bootleggers, law enforcement, and a considerable degree of debauchery. Dorothy invites the Racquet Club, all of the dancers from the Follies, the Prohibitionist Judge Schultzmeyer, and the bootlegger Joe Sanguinetti and his Silver Spray Club, which Lorelei pithily notes "is not even mentioned in the Social Register" (105). The debut is such an event that the celebrity press covers it with rave reviews. Afterward, Lorelei writes: "So my debut has really been very novel, because quite a lot of the guests who finished up at my debut were not the same guests that started out at it, and it really is quite novel for a girl to have so many different kinds of gentlemen at her debut" (106). In this rendering of social space, the debut party corresponds to the revolving door of Koolhaas's hotel, acting not only as setting but also as plot.

The party is noteworthy in that it is deliberately designed to disrupt and distribute social space. During the preparation for the party, Dorothy anticipates that the integration of the Racquet Club and the Silver Spray Club would be a truly distinctive accomplishment: "Dorothy said that by the time the party got into swing, anyone would have to be a genius if he could tell whether he belonged to the Racquet Club, the Silver Spray Club, or the Knights of Pythias" (105). Anyone would have to be a genius, in other words, to separate the partiers into their distinct classes. This is achieved, for example, when the quartet of the Silver Spray Club merges with that of the Racquet Club and the new ensemble quarrels over pieces to perform, as "Joe's bootleggers said that the Racquet club boys wanted to sing songs that were unrefined, while they wanted to sing songs about Mother" (107). The squabble not only obscures class boundaries as the two clubs converge into one unit but also upends traditionally classed assumptions about vulgarity and refinement. Further, the friction between the two Clubs presents the new octet not as a fused unit but as a constellar social body.

Of the debut party, Barreca writes: "Dorothy has created a little pocket of anarchy and gleefully intends to enjoy it" (xiv). The party's subversion of class hierarchy and gender norms is anarchic, to be sure, but it is by no means "a little pocket" of *Blondes*. Rather, it is the general rule of the text, which at nearly every turn seeks to distribute class hierarchy and undo gendered binaries. With *Blondes* and "Cocktail Parties of the Twenties," one suspects that Loos is cultivating a mythology of Prohibition's social milieu—overstating or even fabricating the extent to which the Volstead Act promoted social heterogeneity. Mimesis is not the stake, however. Loos understands these settings instead as sites of wish fulfillment: their distributive functions set them as spaces of radically open social engagement. This reading only emerges in the friction of *Blondes*'s contexts—between Hollywood's massified homogeneity and the class atomization that was hardening throughout the 1920s. Speaking between these two polarities, the text poses a challenge: what if social organization were based on the model of a hotel's public spaces or a cocktail party, where social distribution was the rule instead of classed or gendered boundaries—or even the modern hotel's own racial segregation?

Because they emphasize settings, Loos's distributive public spaces demonstrate the importance of spatial dynamics to the moderns' experiments in network aesthetics. For both Bourne and Toomer, the network's spatial dimensions offer an opportunity to rethink an abstractly understood national space. Loos's space, however, has a more concrete locus because it always carries the referent of setting. Whether the hotel, the cocktail party, or even Fort Loos, these distributed settings gesture toward the spaces of public culture and public exchange that are as constitutive of the cultural logic of modernism as the high modern dialectic of fragment and totality. For *Blondes*, this tension arises between the Hollywood reputations of its author and protagonist and the atomizing class structure that they both chafe against. In turning to referential settings to mediate this tension, *Blondes* offers distributed settings as a material, lived corrective.

4

Schisms

Form and Content, Space and History in John Dos Passos's *U.S.A.* Trilogy

In *1919* (1932), the second volume of his epic trilogy *U.S.A.* (1930–36), John Dos Passos offers a paean to Randolph Bourne. Dos Passos renders Bourne a tragic pariah of American radicalism, concluding with a mythologizing epitaph: "If any man has a ghost / Bourne has a ghost, / a tiny twisted unscared ghost in a black cloak / hopping along the grimy old brick and brownstone streets still left in downtown New York, / crying out in a shrill soundless giggle / *War is the health of the state*" (*1919* 81). Even while Dos Passos's politics were beginning to tilt rightward, *U.S.A.* acknowledges its place in Bourne's legacy of radical critique. This is evident not only in the lionizing tone of Bourne's portrait but also in its placement among the biographical sketches. The thirteenth of the trilogy's twenty-seven biographical portraits, Bourne sits at the median of Dos Passos's profiles of modern American luminaries of thought and industry. The preceding profiles are dominated by labor heroes, such as Eugene Debs, and populists, such as Bob La Follette, and Bourne's sketch is immediately followed by Woodrow Wilson's and then a line of portraits of capitalist magnates, such as Henry Ford and William Randolph Hearst. Bourne's profile, in other words, punctuates a decline-and-fall narrative in the biographical sketches that typifies the broader trajectory of the trilogy's rendering of early twentieth-century American history.

That jeremiad narrative closely attends the trilogy's negotiation of the cultural logic of modernism, much of which takes place in the text's complex form. Built of four autonomous, integrated narrative modes, *U.S.A.* simultaneously asserts totalization and fragmentation as it circumscribes American history from 1900 through the late 1920s. Pairing network aesthetics with this historical project, *U.S.A.* offers something like a constellar model of the study of history. Its sixty-eight Newsreels collate newspaper copy, advertisements, and popular song lyrics to narrate the history and zeitgeist of the period. Its fifty-one Camera Eye passages, which scholars often recognize as a stream-of-consciousness rendering of Dos Passos's own life, narrate the author's lived experience of the period. Its twenty-seven biographical sketches punctuate this history through portraits of figures such as Andrew Carnegie, Thorstein Veblen, the Wright brothers, and Isadora Duncan, the lone woman among these profiles, to explore United States history and culture through their interventions. Its fiction narrates the developments of the period through twelve anchoring character threads. This radical experiment in form complements the radical dissent that runs through the text's critique of the nation. The title of the third book, *The Big Money* (1936), captures Dos Passos's lament that the republic was transforming into an oligarchy.

Although the Bourne portrait situates *U.S.A.* in his genealogy of radical politics, it does not recognize Bourne's other legacy as a progenitor of network aesthetics. This legacy is evident in the distributed function of *U.S.A.*'s form and also in the text's fiction, which is preoccupied with the six-degrees-of-separation formula that Dos Passos had already experimented with in *Manhattan Transfer*. These discrete networks mark two key schisms in the genealogy of modern network aesthetics. One of these is the displacement of utopian social space, which prevails in Bourne's and Jean Toomer's models of distributed community. *U.S.A.* does provide for this dimension, as it deals with the modern tensions between a homogenized, massified national identity and its negation in the fragment. But *U.S.A.*'s form also develops a theory of distributed narration and historical method and thereby fractures modern network aesthetics's heretofore exclusive focus on social space. The other schism derives from the friction between the text's form and its content. The divergence between the form's treatment of narration and historical study and the content's treatment of the six-degrees theory results in a division of labor between form and content. This schism between form and content also makes possible the truncation of contemporary network aesthetics, which privileges the six-degrees scheme as a realist project and largely ignores form as an opportunity to explore distribution. Taken together, these concomitant ruptures—between the substance of the network and between form and content—chart new potential courses for network aesthetics and augur the gutting of modern network aesthetics's profound dynamism.

Form: Distributed Narration

U.S.A.'s quadrangular formal architecture has invited several critical metaphors. Dos Passos referred to it as a "four-way conveyor system" (Denning 170). In *On Native Ground* (1942), Alfred Kazin describes *U.S.A.* as "a conveyor belt carrying Americans through some vast Ford plant of the human spirit" (353). Several recent critics discuss the text in terms of montage. These approaches share a common effort to manage *U.S.A.*'s investment in the high modern dialectic of fragment and totality. Although these metaphors of industrialism and film aptly suit Dos Passos's milieu, the logic of *U.S.A.*'s form is better understood in terms of network aesthetics. The text announces this distribution at the outset: Dos Passos decenters the fiction by introducing it third, behind the first volley of Newsreel and Camera Eye that inaugurate *The 42nd Parallel* (1930), the first of the trilogy. Many of the trilogy's early reviewers chafed at this choice, preferring to treat the Newsreels, Camera Eyes, and biographical sketches as mere white noise included only to reinforce the privileged work of the text's fiction.[1] With the plot- and character-driven narration marginalized from its usual position of authority, *U.S.A.* proceeds to locate its project in the interstices of the four narrative nodes that compose its history of the modern United States.

The most concise demonstration of the text's networked form takes place in *1919*, in which a sequence of each of the four formal registers treats the events of Armistice Day. In the fiction, the action of Armistice Day is related through Joe Williams, whom readers first met as he deserted the merchant marine in Buenos Aires. Joe is in France when the news comes, and he enjoys the exuberant scene: "everybody was dancing in the kitchen and they poured the cook so many drinks he passed out cold and they all sat there singing and drinking champagne out of tumblers and cheering the allied flags that girls kept carrying through" (187). Newsreel XXIX immediately follows, conveying the objective history of the event with headlines reporting the actual signing of the armistice as well as the riotous celebrations that accompanied it: "the arrival of the news caused the swamping of the city's telephone lines"; "at the Custom House the crowd sang The Star Spangled Banner under the direction of Byron R. Newton the Collector of the Port"; "*Oh say can you see by the dawn's early light*"; and so on (189). The thirty-sixth Camera Eye relates the experience of the event: "Hay sojer tell me they've signed an armistice   tell me the wars over they're takin us home latrine talk the hell you say" (191). The biographical sketch at the end of this sequence is a portrait of Woodrow Wilson, and while the armistice itself gets only glancing treatment—"Almost too soon the show was over" (195)—the sketch neatly situates Wilson in the context of the empire building that would be the treaty's legacy. Alongside Clemenceau and Lloyd George, Wilson is one of "three old men shuffling the pack, / dealing out the cards" of imperial mapping (197). Other events unfold in a similar distribution. In consecutive passages of *The 42nd Parallel*, for example, we see the onset of the Great War in Newsreel XV, in a portrait of Andrew Carnegie as a warmonger in the twenty-second Camera Eye, and G. H. Barrow's claim that "this war is America's great opportunity" in a fictional episode featuring J. Ward Moorehouse (213). Only with this division of narrational labor, only in the distribution of these narrative tasks, *U.S.A.* asserts, can these histories be understood.

Jean-Paul Sartre discusses *U.S.A.*'s interstitial semiotics in terms of narrative time. "Chronological order, life's order," he explains, in his essay "John Dos Passos and *1919*" (1947), "barely conceals the causal order, which is an order for the understanding. The event does not touch us; it stands half-way between fact and law" (89). In this passage, Sartre suggests that the text lacks a narrative, or at least any sense of narrative causality. Instead, he says, *U.S.A.* relies on a herky-jerky sensibility akin to memory, with details taking primacy over the Gestalt. Sartre touches on the problems of time that I discuss later in Dos Passos's rendering of historical method, but he also addresses *U.S.A.*'s unique narrational device, in which the text's meaning is produced without squarely confronting an event. Indeed, it is not so much that the event stands between "fact and law," but somewhere in the quadrangulation of Dos Passos's narrative scheme. Although *U.S.A.*'s details often do seem scattered and random, as Sartre reads them, they do not come at the expense of the Gestalt effect produced by the text's four formal registers. This is certainly the narrative principle of the Armistice passage. The event itself is absent from the text, which can only approach it piecemeal from headlines and newspaper copy, from Joe Williams's and the Camera Eye's reactions to the news, and from Wilson's involvement in its aftermath. When I say the text produces its meaning between these formal registers, then, I mean that the rather wide lacunae between them—much like the open spaces inscribed in the distributed form of Toomer's *Cane*—provide readers with several spaces from which to view the unfolding of this history. In other words, *U.S.A.* produces meaning not in any single formal device or even in some combination of the four but in the reader's situation between them.

The open spaces between these formal registers can vary in scale. *The Big Money*, for example, relates the 1927 executions of Nicola Sacco and Bartolomeo Vanzetti—perhaps the most central historical event of the trilogy and a turning point in Dos Passos's affiliations—without the full complement of the trilogy's formal devices. The character Mary French, a social activist working in Boston on behalf of the Italian anarchists, joins a somber protest parade in Charlestown on the day of the executions: "The people she met on the street seemed to look away from her when she passed them. Death watch" (368). Newsreel LXVI follows with headlines calling for the executions, and the fiftieth Camera Eye relays a personal sense of dismay over the event, with the narrator lamenting, "there is nothing left to do   we are beaten   we the beaten" and then uttering the final resignation, perhaps the most famous line of the trilogy: "all right we are two nations" (371). The Sacco and Vanzetti passage, however, strays from the full formal demonstration of the Armistice Day sequence, lacking a biographical portrait that points toward the event from that narrative coordinate. The nearest biography is William Randolph Hearst's, separated from the fiftieth Camera Eye by Newsreel LXVII. Hearst and his papers, famous architects of the Spanish-American War, have nothing to say on the matter of the Italian anarchists. In the absence of a biographical sketch to access the event of the executions, *U.S.A.* creates still more space for the Sacco and Vanzetti event than for Armistice Day—a wide expanse in which readers can approach the unintelligibility of this history.

Still, the distributed narration of events such as Armistice Day or even the Sacco and Vanzetti executions rather oversimplifies *U.S.A.*'s navigation of the fragment/totality binary. The Armistice Day sequence tidily displays the distribution of narrative and the production of meaning between the four formal registers, but the sequence is unrepresentative of the text's architecture, which rarely provides this kind of concise examination of one punctual moment with such tight thematic clustering, uninterrupted by other matters of history and experience that interpenetrate the trilogy, as with the incomplete demonstration of form in the Sacco and Vanzetti passages. Indeed, as Donald Pizer has shown in his important monograph *Dos Passos' U.S.A* (1988), the drafting of the trilogy is itself an index of the tensions in Dos Passos's formal project. On the one hand, Dos Passos drafted each of the narrative modes more or less independently of the others.[2] On the other hand, he did not wait until the drafts were complete to begin thinking about the interplay of the four narrative devices, as his earliest tables of contents demonstrate.[3] Pizer focuses, for instance, on an early outline that sets the character Ike Hall, an automobile worker whose narrative is cut from the final draft of the trilogy and who now only appears as a minor character in Mac's storyline in *The 42nd Parallel*, as a foil to the biographical sketch of Fredrick Winslow Taylor, the father of scientific management. By setting these two figures adjacent to each other, the arrangement of the narrative registers is more thematic than punctual. Moreover, the sum juxtapositions of *U.S.A.*'s narrative modes, as we have seen, are more than binary; they are quadrangular, and thereby produce a more diffuse, more truly constellar narration of the United States' first decades of the new century.

The developing public relations industry better demonstrates the breadth of the trilogy's distributed narration. This development rather eschews the narration of a punctual event that is Sartre's interest but provides another index of the text's interstitial semiotics. The impact of public relations is shown, in part, in the trajectory of the Newsreels across the trilogy. Caren Irr argues in *The Suburb of Dissent* (1998) that the arc of the Newsreels moves from news-related headlines to an array of advertisements that dominate *The Big Money*. The Camera Eye follows this pattern, as brand recognition registers in the stream of consciousness: "walk the streets and walk the streets inquiring of Coca-Cola signs Lucky Strike ads" (118). Curiously, Dos Passos's biographical sketches do not feature a founder of the public relations field—someone such as Ivy Lee or Edward Bernays would not have been surprising—but some of the later sketches do suggest the field's influence. Henry Ford's profile, for example, opens with a glamorizing account by a "featurewriter" whose profile of the auto magnate is equal parts advertisement for Ford and for one of his automobile prototypes: "the machine certainly went with a dreamlike smoothness. There was none of the bumping common even to a streetcar" (38). Alongside the nonfictional narrative modes, J. Ward Moorehouse, the father of public relations in *U.S.A.*'s fictional diegesis and one of many characters working in the field throughout the trilogy, provides a vital thread establishing the importance of public relations in the trilogy's fiction. Although Moorehouse's named chapters expire with the first volume, he has cameos in the chapters featuring Joe Williams and Dick Savage in *1919* and Charley Anderson and

Dick Savage in *The Big Money*. The story of public relations, then, is distributed across the entire span of the trilogy and each of its four narrative devices, multiplying the interstitial sites of meaning production beyond what can be accomplished with one passage's treatment of a discrete event.

In the event of Armistice Day and the diachronic development of public relations, Dos Passos's strategy is the formal distribution of narrative. He does not offer a totalizing history of the United States in which its differences are smoothened under the text's unifying title. Nor does Dos Passos's history assert the fragmentation of its four anchoring narrative devices, as if in a kind of atomized perspectivism. Rather, *U.S.A.*'s treatment of Armistice Day and public relations demonstrates the premium it places on the interdependence of its narrative modes—not their inseparability or their severance. The distribution of the four narrative modes marks the spatial dynamics of a network, which situates each narrative mode nodally in relation to the others. To read any of the narrative modes in isolation unstrings the trilogy's web. *U.S.A.* creates meaning spatially in the linkages or even in the negative spaces between its four narrative modes.

The critical metaphors of Fordism—partly in their recognition of these spatial dimensions and partly in the distributed nature of Fordism itself—approximate this distributed logic more closely than readers might first assume. When Dos Passos and Kazin describe the text with "conveyors" metaphors, or when Michael Denning discusses the trilogy's formal design as an "aesthetic Taylorism" in his seminal book *The Cultural Front* (1997), the text's linear nature comes to the fore. The text's history unfolds in a mostly chronological fashion, and even with its herky-jerky rhythm of narrational modes, readers are not encouraged to read out of order—an important distinction in the study of network aesthetics, given hypertextual fiction's emphasis on its own nonlinearity. For example, the Newsreels start with the dawn of the new century, cover the tumult of the war years, report the first Florida land boom and other hallmarks of the Roaring Twenties, and conclude with the market turmoil that would lead to the Great Depression. And the other narrative modes follow historical chronology, with the fiction presenting minor exceptions in the movement from one dominant character to another that sometimes require a slight reset to establish a character's background.

One intervention of Dos Passos's formal architecture is that its four narrative modes stage a complicated tension between linear and constellar movement, much as the Fordist workplace did in its reliance on subsegmentation. The Fordist paradigm operates on the division of labor, in which separate tasks are performed by separate workers on separate assembly lines. Fordism, then, relies on a process of subsegmentation that yields a complete product only at the end. The product does not take shape incrementally and chronologically. The result is a process that involves autonomy and interdependence, centralized control and dispersed action—the cultural logic of modernism manifested on the factory floor—which suggests distributed rather than linear production. This subsegmented, distributed model is precisely that of *U.S.A.*'s narrative architecture: a division of narrational labor allowing for the independence and autonomy of four distinct narrative tasks.[4] In other words, the form creates a network of narration itself.

These same spatial qualities also undergird the second chief metaphor of *U.S.A.*'s form: montage. As previous chapters have discussed, montage, along with collage, plays a critical role in the development of modern network aesthetics. Dos Passos, of course, has a well-known debt to film. The trilogy's Newsreels are reminiscent of the newsreels edited by Russian filmmaker Dziga Vertov in the *Kino-Pravda* series (1922–25), and in naming one of his narrative modes The Camera Eye, Dos Passos invokes Vertov's "kino-eye," an avant-garde philosophy of montage performed in *Man with a Movie Camera* (1929). In "Early Soviet Cinema and American Poetry" (2004), David Kadlec observes that by the mid-thirties Dos Passos's debt to Vertov was widely recognized among the literati and that Vertov was proud to be known for influencing Dos Passos.[5] Still more broadly, D. W. Griffith's innovations in crosscutting and the epic influenced Dos Passos's stylistic and formal experiments in such early works as *Three Soldiers* (1921) and *Manhattan Transfer* and continued to manifest in *U.S.A.*, as Lisa Nanney shows in her trenchant monograph, *John Dos Passos Revisited* (1998).[6] The metaphor, then, charts a comparative study of influence, as well as the circulation of montage across forms and hemispheres. The shared project of montage situates these artists, their nations, and their forms in the transnational emergence of modern network aesthetics.

Beyond the appeal of biographical criticism, montage prevails in *U.S.A.* scholarship because, like the Fordism metaphors, it grasps at the text's spatial dimensions. For example, in *Shifting Gears* (1987) Cecelia Tichi invokes montage as she argues that Dos Passos's "omniscient fictional form comes from the contemporary model of machine and structural technology" (216).

Irr, writing about the collisions that underlie *U.S.A.*'s performance of social speed, also confronts the issue of montage. Observing the many literal collisions of cars and airplanes in the text, she notes the logic of collision at the formal level: Dos Passos "constructs montages whose organizing principle is the collision between these equally inadequate modes of writing" (64). In emphasizing collisions between the trilogy's "equally inadequate" narrative modes, Irr brings montage to bear not on the trilogy's filmic qualities but rather the spatial dynamics of its autonomous narratives, their lines and their points of convergence.

Montage provides a helpful analogy for the text and rightly demonstrates Dos Passos's interest in film, but it does not fully engage the distributive logic of *U.S.A.*'s form—not, at least, without a deeper study of the formal properties of montage. An emphasis on modern network aesthetics illuminates the formal logic of montage and provides a richer context for understanding Dos Passos's formal experiments. Whereas the Fordist conveyor belt emphasizes linearity, montage creates meaning both in its diachronic sequence of images and in the synchronic juxtaposition of images within the same frame. In the montage experiments of modern film and even the photography and advertisements that experimented with the advent of half-tone printing in the 1880s,[7] old meanings are overturned and new meanings are produced by different techniques such as sequential revolutions, overlays, split images, and mirrored images. Whether in the synchronic images of a single frame or the diachronic procession of multiple frames, montage's productive capacity is often held to lie in the collisions it creates, in the violent contrast of juxtaposed images. This is the force of montage for Irr, who reads *U.S.A.*'s four narrative modes as operating on an organizational principle of collision.

As with earlier chapters' discussions of collage, montage produces meaning not only by juxtaposition but also in the coordination of images and in the negative spaces between them. Such coordination is, after all, evoked in Dos Passos's metaphor of the "four-way conveyor system." The four modes of narration are distinct, to be sure, but they produce meaning in their distributed, coordinated—not colliding or disjunctive—narration of history, as in the Armistice Day sequence and other developments and events that fall under the trilogy's scope. *U.S.A.*'s narration has the multidimensional force of montage, but the logic of its productive capacity is fundamentally different from the theories and practices of montage that rely on collision. Disjunctive montage and networked montage both operate on a constellar model, but networked montage allows a degree of totalization, if not exactly coherence. And this distributed montage may be uniquely American. In contrast to the European and Russian experiments with montage, Christopher Phillips argues that, by the late 1930s in the United States, "montage was more and more recognized not as a means to evoke the flux and discontinuity of the modern world, but as a way to represent a dominant social theme in late Depression America: the idea of the 'unity in diversity' of all classes and ethnic groups" (35). Phillips responds to American trends in the visual arts, but Dos Passos's trilogy follows the same path, emphasizing the networked interdependence of the separate narrative modes instead of their stark disconnections.

Situating *U.S.A.* amid the moderns' network aesthetics demonstrates the weaknesses in the trilogy's prevailing critical metaphors and illuminates the text's formal logic of interconnection, while allowing readers to see in *U.S.A.* the playing out of the cultural logic of American modernism. It is insufficient merely to observe that *U.S.A.*'s representational strategy fits tidily into one of the now standard narratives of the moderns' revolt against verisimilitude or that it lifts its techniques from avant-garde montage. Instead, *U.S.A.*'s form displays the emergence of distributed models in American modernism. In this narrative work, *U.S.A.* provides a pivot from earlier moderns' focus on social space, mobilizing network models to a study of narration itself.

Content: Six-Degrees Fiction

Underneath this radical distribution of narration in its form, *U.S.A.* engages another model of network aesthetics in its content through the six-degrees formations of its characters. The fictional element of what Dos Passos called *U.S.A.*'s "reportages of the time" remained at the core of his understanding of the trilogy (Ludington 256). According to biographer Townsend Ludington, the trilogy's fiction weighed just a bit more than other narrative modes for Dos Passos, who expected *U.S.A.* would be "not a novel, but a series covering a lengthy period, 'in which characters appeared and reappeared'" (256). Although the trilogy incorporates nonfiction, Dos Passos assigned a special role to its fiction. It was through fiction, Dos Passos wrote, that the history of the period could be "seen by some individual's ears, felt by some individual's nerves and tissues" (Ludington 256). But it is only through a distributed corpus of characters that the lived experience of the period could be represented.

Reflecting the major developments of the period that are distributed across *U.S.A.*'s form, the fictional characters serve as secondary nodes under the primary nodal construction of the trilogy's four narrative modes, providing a comfortable fictional body through which the historical and social developments resonate. In *The 42nd Parallel*, J. Ward Moorehouse provides a face for the developments in public relations, and several others, for instance, G. H. Barrow and Dick Savage, carry that banner throughout the remainder of the trilogy. Joe Williams charts the tumultuous war years in *1919*, and Ben Compton does the same for labor movements during that period. Charley Anderson and Margo Dowling give voice to the "roar" of the debt-fueled Roaring Twenties throughout *The Big Money*. And the other key characters generally perform the same function, reinforcing the trilogy's historical commentary with a handy synecdoche for the period's major developments. Read this way, the network of characters is subordinated to the larger project of *U.S.A.*'s distributed form—despite what Dos Passos may have thought of the primacy of the trilogy's fiction.

In addition to linking to the text's larger formal architecture, the characters are distributed across the social space of the novel, connecting to each other in six degrees-of-separation fashion.[8] With its characters' appearances and reappearances, *U.S.A.*'s fiction anticipates David Bordwell's pronouncement of the "network narrative" genre, which arrives at the end of the century and features ensembles of crisscrossing characters. As in the contemporary films Bordwell studies, Dos Passos's characters are largely unaware of their own interconnections, and the reader does the work of drawing the network of lines that connect them out of their physical intersections, their social transactions, or, more loosely, their situation of thematic likeness. Doc Bingham, one of the trilogy's most colorful characters, demonstrates this principle of appearance and reappearance, gathering and diverging. Bingham is a minor character, never enjoying the spotlight of a chapter titled after his name. Instead, he only surfaces in the fictional segments "Mac" in *The 42nd Parallel* and "Richard Ellsworth Savage" in *The Big Money*. His appearance alongside Fenian "Mac" McCreary is brief but memorable. Mac answers a want ad listed for The Truthseeker Literary Distributing Co., Inc., by Emmanuel R. Bingham, D.D. The pair travels the countryside posing as purveyors of moral pamphlets, but

Bingham is quick to advertise other, less pious wares. Bingham stocks such scandalous tracts as *The Queen of the White Slaves* and tells one mark: "We have a number of very interesting books stating the facts of life frankly and freely, describing the deplorable licentiousness of life in the big cities, ranging from a dollar to five dollars. *The Complete Sexology of Dr. Burnside,* is six fifty" (*42nd* 36). The con is up, however, when Bingham is caught in bed with a patron's wife and abandons Mac to fend for himself. He disappears before the first volume of the trilogy has hardly begun. He does not resurface until deep into *The Big Money*, when Dick Savage is assigned to handle a public relations account for Bingham, now going by "E. R. Bingham," whose latest scam involves alternative medication and diets. Again, the con man's appearance is fleeting. Bingham, the advocate of clean living, convinces Savage to escort him around some of the city's seedy sex districts and eventually grants him the account. His only subsequent appearance in the text is indirect: Savage and the Moorehouse public relations firm lobby on his behalf for food legislation and arrange favorable publicity on radio and newsreels.[9]

This six-degrees formation mediates modernism's trademark polarities of fragmentation and totalization in the content of *U.S.A.* Michael Denning voices a concern for the former, lamenting the text's disaggregated social space. Bingham himself is a token of this disaggregation. His reemergence alongside Dick Savage, more than a thousand pages after he abandoned Mac, may strike readers as frivolous, and it is the kind of detail in six-degrees narratives that for many smacks of contrivance. Bingham typifies Denning's criticism that *U.S.A.*'s social space remains a jumble of disconnections—a critique that was common among the trilogy's first reviewers. "Perhaps the most striking and unsettling aspect of *U.S.A.*," Denning writes, "is the lack of any coherent connection between the characters: no family or set of families constitutes the world of the novel; no town, neighborhood, or city serves as a knowable community; no industry or business, no university or film colony unites public and private lives; and no plot, murder, or inheritance links the separate destinies" (*Cultural Front* 182). Bingham's weak ties to primary figures such as Mac and Dick Savage substantiate Denning's concerns, as he has no family or community ties to bind him to other characters. In fact, his wandering lifestyle may make Bingham one of the most fully disaggregated of all of *U.S.A.*'s characters. His social isolation is reinforced by his complete marginalization from the plots of the trilogy's fiction. Bingham is unnecessary to demonstrate

Savage's loyalty to the Moorehouse firm and to advance his eventual fall from grace, which one might assume are Dos Passos's primary reasons for dragging Savage through strip clubs and Bingham's incessant claptrap.

This disaggregated social space relies on contingency. Typified by appearances and reappearances, meetings and departures, the text's nodal exchanges take place by chance. For instance, throughout the trilogy G. H. Barrow displays improbably wide and inclusive social contacts, intersecting with "Mac" McCreary, stenographer Janey Williams, Dick Savage, the wandering Anne Elizabeth "Daughter" Trent, labor advocate Mary French, activist Ben Compton, and aspiring actress Margo Dowling. These intersections are often cursory and brief. For example, at the last of Eveline Hutchins's cocktail parties—indeed, the party that concludes *The Big Money*—Mary French briefly glimpses the starlet Margo Dowling. French's profile thus far has centered on her social activism through Hull House and her advocacy for Sacco and Vanzetti, and Dowling has been something of a foil character, self-involved and materialistic in her fervent pursuit of stardom. The connection is a fleeting one: "Mary saw a small woman with blue eyelids and features regular as those of a porcelain doll under a mass of paleblond hair turn for a second to smile at somebody before she went out through the sliding doors" (442). Mary and Margo are not introduced and have no substantive awareness of each other, but readers recognize Margo's description and register the weak tie that flashes precariously between them. Without any more meaningful bonds between these characters, the text lends itself to a reading of atomized social space—the very failure, as Denning notes, of knowable community.

The lack of intimacy between Mary French and Margo Dowling is at the heart of what many criticize as disorganization, disaggregation, or atomization in the trilogy's fiction. Without a shared community, without a common relation to an ongoing plot, and without so much as an introduction, it is hard to see any connection between the two women. In fact, the only thing they have in common is Eveline Hutchins, their mediating link. Whatever connections there are between these characters, there is rarely enough to constitute a knowable community. Even in the case of family, most characters carry a high degree of estrangement. Joe Williams, Dick Savage, "Daughter" Trent, Ben Compton, Charley Anderson, Margo Dowling, Mary French—nearly all the major characters are deeply alienated from their biological families in one way or another. With only weak ties among these characters, the text lends itself to a reading of atomized social space in which any shared experience is contingent, cursory, and inconsequential, making a knowable community unattainable.

Countering the problem of social dispersal, however, *U.S.A.*'s content emphasizes homogenizing institutions that totalize social space and that therefore pose a different threat to the project of community formation. Just as the Newsreels slowly shift from news to advertisements, the fiction increasingly focuses on the hegemonic functions of industry. This trajectory is punctuated by the title of the third book; "the big money," a phrase that also circulates below the title, refers generally to American capital, often specifically invoking the culture industries embodied by Hollywood.[10] *U.S.A.*'s fiction narrates this totalization in the rise of public relations, registered in the J. Ward Moorehouse and Dick Savage passages; in the growth of mass media, which is especially prominent in Margo Dowling's rendering of Hollywood's sterility; and in capital's ascendancy over the labor movement during the so-called Coolidge Prosperity, figured by Charley Anderson.[11] Charley, whose passages dominate *The Big Money*, is in many ways the avatar of big business. Having served in the Great War as an airman, Charley works his way into the aviation industry as a mechanic and becomes a sought-after engineer for prestigious manufacturers. As he becomes an executive in the Tern manufacturing company, he also enjoys success playing at stocks. But his great successes give way to equally intense failures. A trading gambit batters his investments: "by the end of the week, he'd lost four hundred thousand dollars and had let go every airplane stock he had in the world" (257). He is precariously overinvested in the Florida land boom, which is also the subject of several Newsreel clippings in *The Big Money*. And Dos Passos indicates that from the beginning Charley has paid for his decadent lifestyle on credit. Even as a corporate executive he borrows twenty thousand dollars—"what with the hospital expenses and the furniture bills and Christmas" (244). In both his personal finances and in his business deals, Charley is the model of American capital in the 1920s: debt, speculation, volatility.

As a marker of big business, Charley signals a totalized social space that is the antithesis of the disaggregation observed by Denning. As with the homogenizing function of mass media, big business augurs, to borrow Alan Trachtenberg's phrase, the incorporation of America—the enclosure of national space under a single, monolithic system. In "Masscult and Midcult" Dwight Macdonald registers the moderns' concern over such totalized space in their treatment of the culture industry. Macdonald argues that the high moderns' staple critique is as much about Hollywood's degraded aesthetics as it is about the social formations it yields. His suspicion of "mass industry" and one of its signal byproducts, mass culture, would lead Macdonald to assert the impossibility of cultural pluralism during this period—the chief obstacle, he felt, to Bourne's transnationalism thesis (34). The same principle holds in suspicion of robber-baron capital, which *U.S.A.* demonstrates in all four of its narrative modes. Big business's blind rapaciousness not only widens an already dire wealth gap. It also portends an undesirably uniform, massified social space in which the nation is made in its likeness. In other words, although the fiction seems to quash meaningful ties in its atomized social space, its totalizing institutions likewise distress the possibility of any recognizable form of community—knowable or otherwise.

The stresses to social space that preoccupy Macdonald's criticism are similar to those that motivate Jean-Paul Sartre's discussion of group formations in his *Critique of Dialectical Reason* (1960). Like Macdonald, Sartre is concerned with the mediations that shape social space. He studies three types of social mediations that hang in dialectical suspension with each other. "Seriality" is a state in which individuals are linked together by a chain of others who share a common interest; this group formation bears the most similarity to *U.S.A.*'s atomized social space and also echoes Jules Romains's unanimisme in its urban contexts.[12] Whereas the series is united by a common interest, the "fused group" shares an action; crowds and mobs demonstrate this social formation and could well yield a collective if it were not for their temporal limitations. The "institution" develops from a pledged group into an organized group, often featuring a sovereign authority, and finally becomes structurally ossified; dominated by keywords such as "pledge" and "purge" and "terror," Sartre's study of the institution hints at the potential horrors that could arise when such a mediator becomes fully external to its creators and rules over them. Sartre's description of the institution parallels Macdonald's description of industries of mass culture; indeed, they share a critique of social space arbitrated by an outside party. In Sartre's view, the institution is one form of mediation among three that are dialectically entangled. The fused group remains a series, he writes, although one in which there is no differentiation between self and group and in which the institution shares seriality's inability to determine action by itself.

Critically, for Sartre, each of these group formations forecloses the possibility of a true common, collective experience—a more damning articulation of the closures of social space, perhaps, than Macdonald's. Whereas seriality is organized by a common need, the fused group by a common action, and the institution by a common objective, each fails to produce a community "by feeling individual need as common need" (*Critique* 350). However, between its polarities of failed community—disaggregated weak ties, monolithic capital—*U.S.A.*'s fiction proposes distributed social space as a pathway toward such a common experience. If the frequency of contingent exchanges such as Doc Bingham's is any indication, the trilogy does not altogether reject the premise of life in common. Rather, *U.S.A.*'s fiction imagines what community might look like on a distributed model. In other words, the characters are not disaggregated but reaggregated as a network. To say that these characters do not realize their interconnection is not to say that they are, in fact, disconnected. Denning is right to observe that the trilogy mostly disregards family, neighborhood, work, and so on as foundations of social organization. But its six-degrees networks create a new basis of organization—one that is purely interpersonal, without constraints of place or institution. The six-degrees model forfeits the strong ties of kinship or place-based communities, but its weak ties should not be confused with outright social entropy. Instead, this distributed model of social organization marks the replacement of the conventional communities associated with realism and thus marks an important, inherently modernist reformulation of the nation that decentralizes national space to rearticulate notions of community, rootedness, and belonging in the space between fragmentation and totalization.

Searching for a vestige of realist social coherence in the trilogy, Denning concludes that the fundamental social unit of *U.S.A.* is the cocktail party. The cocktail party, he writes, "stands as a substitute for narratives of home and family, an alternative to the domestic space that usually organizes the novel. . . . In *U.S.A.*, the party is not only a social structure and a symbolic space, it is a narrative kernel, one of the basic building blocks of the novel" (*Cultural Front* 183). This work is performed largely by the socialite Eveline Hutchins—and more broadly, in the figurative cocktail party of "illassorted people," to use one of Hutchins's phrases, who populate the trilogy (*Big Money* 444). For Denning, this setting localizes the text's general logic of social disaggregation. To whatever extent the characters interrelate in a shared place, Denning argues, their fundamental disconnections outweigh the ligatures that hold them together.

And yet the cocktail party itself illustrates the networked logic of *U.S.A.*'s social space, as the previous chapter on Anita Loos's distributed settings explores in further detail. Denning grants that this setting fosters exchanges across class divides, bridging "the young men and women on the way up, out for 'the big money'" as well as those who are slumming (183). But even this yields a fraudulent, insincere means of social organization, for the slumming partygoers have no desire for lasting ties to an exotic, working Other. Rather, Denning writes, slumming "is not finally a depiction of the working-class districts; it is a depiction of those who seek them out" (198). Because these cocktail parties are so heavily invested in slumming, Denning argues, they are little more than a reinforcement of a privileged, homogeneous class position; the outward gaze of slumming deconstructs itself, foreclosing the very difference it purportedly seeks out. Again, it is the weak tie that for Denning subverts any possibility of meaningful community. But for better or worse, *U.S.A.*'s fiction relies on the weak-tie dynamics of the six-degrees formation as its fundamental unit of social space. And this is reflected in the organizing principle of the trilogy's cocktail parties. Although Denning is right to be suspicious of the ethical quandaries involved in slumming, slumming does not undermine the social organization produced by this particular setting. The cocktail party does not reinforce an unbreachable, homogeneous class stratum but instead localizes the heterogeneous weak ties and distributed social formation of the six-degrees theory that prevail throughout the trilogy's fiction. This is the payoff, for example, of the fleeting glance between Mary French and Margo Dowling at Eveline's soirée—the convergence of six-degrees organization and the cocktail party setting.

This is all to say that Denning's critique of the trilogy's disaggregated social space is better understood as a concern about the nature of the strength of tie and not about the lack of organic connections throughout Dos Passos's fiction. Strong ties and weak ties, of course, determine different degrees of affinity and solidarity and therefore produce different measures of community. A social milieu built entirely of weak-tie relations may facilitate a wider range of knowledges and experiences, but it comes at the expense of a strong tie's deeper knowability. But it is precisely this distributed, weak-tie social space that *U.S.A.* asserts as a negotiation of the dialectical tensions of fragment and totality—in other words, as the very condition of the modern and as the premise of the period's commons. To locate a "substitute for narratives of home and family" in order to organize *U.S.A.*'s diegesis, as Denning does with the cocktail party, is a false projection of a traditionally ordered narrative. More specifically, it is to insist on the conventions of realism—not only its emphasis on verisimilitude but also its assertion that a complex social milieu could be rendered coherently. Instead, Dos Passos's modernist intervention is to challenge readers to make sense of disaggregation on its own terms and to reorder their assumptions about social coherence.

Precisely because the six-degrees formation eschews realism's more coherent, strong-tie relations, such as kinship or place-based community, it suggests a flattening of the social sphere. In other words, without relational determinants, these characters mix freely and are able to invent new affiliations and new social formations. It is hard to imagine another context in which an activist such as Mary French—who at any rate is not slumming but is a true labor advocate—and a rising star such as Margo would share the same space. Thus, Eveline's dedication to gathering together "illassorted people," bourgeois as it is in her practice, also carries the potential of creating new groups that her politics cannot control and that might well subvert hierarchies of class, race, work, and gender in ways that she cannot anticipate. None of this is to say that such networks of "illassorted people" reliably produce new affiliations, as Denning's concerns about disaggregation indicate. But they do accentuate the possibility of new social formations rising out of radically flattened social organization, fitting the genealogy Bourne established for the utopian impulse of modern network aesthetics.

If *U.S.A.*'s fiction celebrates distribution as an approximation of the common, however, it does not follow that a collective life is its byproduct. In this regard, I think Denning's critique of disaggregated social space hits its mark. Indeed, the project of collective life is fully negated in the Camera Eye's disgust and resignation at the Sacco and Vanzetti executions, registered in the famous lamentation, "all right we are two nations." And still further for this study, the "two nations" pronouncement may well negate the projects of modern network aesthetics. After all, how could such constellations take hold, let alone thrive, in a world organized around such an indelible binary?

The challenge of "two nations" is another indicator of the struggles to define national and social space that we have seen since Bourne's "Trans-National America" and the classed group formations that are the focus of the following study of Nathanael West's fiction. For Bourne, the task is to negotiate calls for a national identity based on the melting pot and those organized as a striated cultural pluralism—between a smoothly homogeneous state and a collection of enclaves that scarcely intersect. Dos Passos's binary seems still more stubborn than Bourne's preparedness discourses, likely because they refer to a structure of class power that is so durable as to seem insuperable. The fiftieth Camera Eye asserts this binary from start to finish, beginning, "they have clubbed us off the streets they are stronger they are rich" and concluding, "we stand defeated America" (371, 372). Whereas competing theories of social space carry ideological or ideational force, Dos Passos's "two nations" binary is enforced also with a violent exercise of power. Read one way, *U.S.A.*'s six-degrees milieu might produce another distributed corrective to the binary of American class stratification, similar to the lived settings of Anita Loos's *Gentlemen Prefer Blondes* that defy the widening and hardening wealth gap of that period. Another reading, however, holds that *U.S.A.*'s reassertion of class polarization against the distributed social space of its fiction demonstrates the stubbornness not only of class structure but also of class consciousness. In this way, the Camera Eye's assertion of "two nations" marks a key failure to produce the collective out of the connective. The inability of modern network aesthetics to effect such a transformation haunts our aesthetic production and political imaginary today.

Rupture: A Departure from Utopian Distributed Space

U.S.A. marks both continuity and discontinuity in the field of modern network aesthetics, in some ways because of the friction between the flattened social formation of its six-degrees fiction and the persistence of class hierarchy in its "two nations" thesis. The distributed social geography of the trilogy's fiction aligns with Bourne's utopian understanding of networks, which emerged in response to the crises of the prewar period. In the content of its fiction, in other words, *U.S.A.* is haunted by Bourne's "ghost," even if for another reason than his biographical sketch in *1919* suggests; the trilogy is an inheritor of Bourne's manifesto of distributed social space, in addition to carrying the banner of his radical dissent. The trilogy's form, however, applies its distributed models inwardly, using them to theorize the nature of narration itself and having little, if any, investment in questions of social life. The form's indifference to utopian politics—keyed, perhaps, by acquiescence to the social space of "two nations"—is all the more vivid when contrasted with the social allegory of form in Toomer's *Cane*. Ultimately, rather than suggesting a complementary interplay of form and content, the double register of networks creates friction and indicates a schism in modern network aesthetics between utopian models of social space and less directly political applications of distributed models, which in *U.S.A.*'s case are concerned with narration and history.

Having relegated its treatment of social space to one corner of its formal architecture, *U.S.A.* intervenes in network aesthetics by using distributed models to rethink the work of history. This, of course, marks a major departure from Bourne and his forebears, moving from direct political engagement toward a theoretical reflection on method itself—an unexpected shift, given the trilogy's reputation for radical politics. This theory of history remains radical in itself, but in a way that largely eschews the utopian zeal that defines the emergent tradition of modern network aesthetics. For Denning, the substance of the trilogy resides in the treatment of history by its form, a reading that comports with Dos Passos's conception of the trilogy as "a series of reportages of the time." Denning argues that each mode of narration corresponds to a distinct register of history: the Newsreels are a sort of public history; the Camera Eye performs the work of memory; the biographical sketches offer a grand narrative of the period; and the fiction narrates "a tale of capital" (*Cultural Front* 170–72). Fordist subsegmentation then provides a model not only for narration but also of historical analysis. This formulation works especially well for Denning's argument that *U.S.A.* narrates the decline and fall of the Lincoln republic and even obtains if one is reading the trilogy as a kind of historical documentary.

But differentiating among the historical methods of the narrative modes could be still more precise in illuminating *U.S.A.*'s pivotal position in modern network aesthetics. To do so means teasing out the specific kinds of work performed by each of Dos Passos's "four-way conveyors." The Newsreels, as Irr has shown, turn more and more from news reporting to advertisements. The role of the Camera Eye progressively diminishes. There are twenty-seven in *The 42nd Parallel*, fifteen in *1919*, and only nine in *The Big Money*, showing a demotion of the importance of interiority throughout the trilogy. The fiction moves toward decay and corruption, emphasizing failure with the conclusion of each character's thread: Charley Anderson dies of peritonitis; Margo Dowling cannot make the jump into talkies and is headed for obscurity; Dick Savage, signaling the bankruptcy of his character, prepares to take over J. Ward

Moorehouse's public relations firm; and Mary French is so disillusioned with her social work that she considers suicide. The biographical sketches chart a similar path, progressively focusing less on thinkers, inventors, and labor heroes, and more on monopolists and captains of industry. The correspondence of the narrative modes' trajectories toward a state of ruins demonstrates that they share a common project—to narrate the replacement of the Lincoln republic with an oligarchy. But it takes another step to discern what exactly each narrative mode is doing to advance that project. The Newsreels consider the problem of the apparatus of culture and its complicity in the rise of a new consumer society. The Camera Eye focuses on subjectivity and illustrates its diminishment in an age of reification. The fiction narrates the struggles of workers, though it would be hard to characterize all of them as working-class given the diversity of work performed by the various figures. And the biographical sketches aggrandize the ruling class: captains of industry ascend over inventors, thinkers, and artists to become the "great men" of the period. In each case, the narrative mode operates within the boundaries of one corner or another of the politics of capital. In other words, *U.S.A.*'s networks are not only concerned with American history in the early twentieth century but also with the very project of historical-materialist analysis. In this light, its distributed form retains a radical charge, if not a direct focus on social space.

Such an approach to the study of history is not without precedent among Dos Passos's contemporaries. Walter Benjamin, whose oeuvre routinely invokes the figure of the constellation, explores the distributed nature of history in several of his later works. For example, in "Theses on the Philosophy of History," written shortly before his tragic suicide, Benjamin cautions against causal relations in historical study.[13] As a result, Benjamin favors a distributed, rather than linear, understanding of history: "A historian who takes this as his point of departure stops telling the sequence of events like the beads of a rosary. Instead, he grasps the constellation which his own era has formed with a definite earlier one" (263). For Benjamin, the study of history is not the ossification of a continuum of inevitable events but a study of the breaks and disjunctures of history as well as the ligatures that give it shape.

This dynamic understanding of history is also evident in *The Arcades Project*, the posthumously published exercise in what Benjamin described as "literary montage." Drawing on the networked organization of montage, Benjamin calls for a constellar methodology of historical materialism to take root in the

Marxist tradition, as discussed in the introduction. To grasp the construction of history, Benjamin writes, one must first "carry over the principle of montage into history," breaking from "vulgar historical naturalism" by locating in the discrete moment "the crystal of the total event" (461). Again, Benjamin's program is to conceive of history not as a linear narrative of progress or decline but as a constellar assembly of various paths taken and abandoned across time. Benjamin's theory of history is symptomatic of the dialectic of modernism, refusing a monolithic narrative of history and instead relying on networked models to mediate the false unity implied in narrative linearity.

Benjamin provides the expository demonstration of this networked theory of history, whereas Dos Passos implements it in aesthetics. This model rejects linearity and its implication of inevitability, turning the focus of study to alternate paths that might have been taken. It allows for counterfactuals that would have appealed to Dos Passos in his lament for the Lincoln republic—for instance, Randolph Bourne's ghost haunting the radical politics that never fully seized the American public—or to Benjamin in his hope that fascism might be overcome, perhaps by communism. And for both writers a distributed history comports with their radical politics, especially in its ability to deny capital's rhetoric of inevitability. *U.S.A.* does demonstrate some linearity in the coordinated narrative of decline, ruin, and failure. And anyway the trilogy never indulges in an outright counterfactual fantasy. But in the interstices of its four modes of narration—in other words, in the negative space of its network of form—the trilogy affirms the gaps, omissions, and false starts that are elided in a smoothly linear narrative account of history. In honoring these interstitial paths and others as equally viable directions of a networked system, the trilogy aligns with Benjamin's theory of constellar history.

Despite the trilogy's linear decline-and-fall narrative, and despite the common critique that it is a work of defeatism, it would be wrong to conclude that *U.S.A.*'s networked model of history appeals only to history's "losers." Instead, this distributed method gets at the texture of history and privileges the breadth of lived experience over the post hoc nature of narrativization that strives for a single, linear narrative thread. That commitment to the texture and multitudinousness of history drives *U.S.A.*'s work as a "series of reportages of the time." And it is a thorough project, matching Benjamin's rejection of linear history in the trilogy's rejection of narrative linearity. But this distributed model also inscribes onto historical analysis the central dialectical tension of modernism, setting history as a field of play between the polarities of unity and dispersal.

Benjamin's project "to carry over the principle of montage into history" aimed to displace "vulgar historical naturalism" with a distributed principle that would be better suited to the modern period. Indeed, *U.S.A.* proves equal to the task, making the montage of history its primary intervention into network aesthetics. But in the bargain, the trilogy subordinates a utopian rendering of social space to the theory of distributed history—a theory that remains radical, but with an entirely different application than the modern network aesthetics that preceded *U.S.A.* This schism marks a fateful break from Bourne's manifesto and makes possible the depoliticization of network aesthetics later in the century.

Rupture: A Departure from Form

Closely attending the treatment of social space in modern network aesthetics is a rupture in its treatment of form as a privileged vehicle for imagining distribution. *U.S.A.* stands apart from Toomer's *Cane*, where, as chapter 2 has shown, the allegory of form is the device by which Toomer imagines a distributed social space against the segregation and hierarchy of Jim Crow's national space. *U.S.A.*'s dual register of networks produces another schism: in addition to separating the substance of the network—separating, in other words, social space from historical method—the trilogy also rends the work of form from that of content. With this division in place, *U.S.A.* paves the way for the six-degrees theory to operate today with virtually nothing invested in formal experiment. The schism leads directly to David Bordwell's identification of the "network narrative genre" in contemporary film, where the network is comprised of characters alone.

This schism invites scholars to consider an alternate literary history—an invitation that comports with *U.S.A.*'s theory of distributed history. The formal inventions of today's literary network aesthetics seem restricted to the hypertextual narratives of "network fiction" studied by David Ciccoricco. What has caused this general abandonment of the moderns' formal interventions into network aesthetics? And what would Bordwell's network narrative genre look like if this attention to form were restored, if the schism were undone? The rupture in the treatment of form in modern network aesthetics opens onto broader questions of modernism. For instance, what happened to the moderns' spirit of formal experimentation—not only in the set of late century films that Bordwell studies but also in late modern and contemporary narrative generally?

Dos Passos's oeuvre is not altogether representative of this rejection of formal innovation. He continued to adapt *U.S.A.*'s formal architecture into the late modern period with *Midcentury* (1960) and the posthumously published *Century's Ebb*.[14] Although his rightward shift fits the political contexts of the late moderns, his insistence on formal experiment made him something of an outlier.[15] His continued experiments with form, however, are something of an exception proving the rule of late modernism, where the swerve away from form holds in both network aesthetics and in narrative generally.

Indeed, it is not so much that formal experimentation was abandoned by the late moderns. A raft of abstract expressionist experiments in pure form indicates quite the contrary. But the late moderns do generally refuse a form that signifies other than itself—a motivated form, an allegorical form such as *Cane*'s or *U.S.A.*'s. In *A Singular Modernity* (2002), his indispensable study of modernity and modernisms, Fredric Jameson writes that abstract expressionism's leashing of form is a signal of the core ideology of late modernism. Late modernism, for Jameson, is "the theory of art, the ideology of modernism, which it was the very role of abstract expressionism pre-eminently to have generated and which then accompanied it everywhere abroad as a specifically North American cultural imperialism" (168). In poetry, Jameson maintains, late modernism demands the substitution of Wallace Stevens's complexities for T. S. Eliot's and Ezra Pound's tarnishing politics.

As an immediate precursor to this period, *U.S.A.* demonstrates that form always carries one politics or another. This, perhaps, explains the reduction to content in contemporary network aesthetics—the truncation of the moderns' full range of distributed devices to the six-degrees formula. In one sense, form might be perceived as obsolete to network aesthetics if content shows itself capable of doing the work of distribution, as it does in the six-degrees scheme. The abandonment of formal experiments such as *U.S.A.*'s, however, testifies not only to the politics of form, which the late moderns were eager to quash, but also to the political value of the network itself. As the introduction discusses, this value is disputed by many contemporary network thinkers. For instance, Alexander R. Galloway and Eugene Thacker argue in *The Exploit* that the network model has no inherent politics at all—liberatory, reactionary, or otherwise. But the late modern purge of this particular type of form, even while it would allow the six-degrees theory to continue in content, suggests otherwise. And this should cast some doubt on whatever weak-tie politics the sequestered six-degrees theory lays claim to, especially in light of the challenge posed by the indelible class binary of the United States' "two nations." *U.S.A.*'s schisms put on full display the forceful critiques of modern network aesthetics and make visible the suppressions and truncations of postwar and contemporary narrative.

5

Nathanael West's Crowds and the Closure of Modern Network Aesthetics

Having failed to find a place among the expatriates during his 1926 sojourn in Paris and later in the Greenwich Village scene of Mike Gold and Edmund Wilson, Nathanael West settled in the coterie of writers who met at the Stanley Rose Bookstore on Hollywood Boulevard. Rose made space for exhibitions of contemporary art and also for a salon of writers to meet and discuss literature. West never enjoyed great critical or financial success with the studios or with his novels, but at Rose's he was a figure of some distinction. He convened with such high modern luminaries as William Faulkner, who would later take West on hunting excursions; F. Scott Fitzgerald, who acted as a mentor to West; and Dashiell Hammett, Horace McCoy, John O'Hara, and others who had come to work in Hollywood during the 1930s. For West and the others at Rose's salon, the bookstore was understood as a sanctuary from the drudgery and degradation of studio life.

But for West, the bookstore served another function, too, by providing him contacts to Los Angeles's underworld. West's biographer Jay Martin describes Rose as "a frustrated confidence man": he spent a year in jail for pirating a copy of a Chick Sale book; he seems to have circulated pornography out of the bookshop; and he often ran slot machines out of the back (270). Rose's shop attracted an array of ex-bootleggers and small-time gangsters, and West was keen to exploit them for material on the life of the masses. Rose, who receives a passing mention in *The Day of the Locust*, West's most famous work, facilitated a convergence of the high moderns and the very masses that they often defined themselves against. The bookstore demonstrates one of the central tensions of West's fiction—between the avant-garde and the popular—and stages the familiar cultural logic of modernism in the assertion of and resistance to massified culture.

West's situation in the culture industry comes as no surprise to his readers, given his consistent engagement with studio settings, mass media, the masses themselves, and crowds. Indeed, these figures are often fused in West's fiction, as well as its criticism. The masses and the crowd are routinely conflated, blurring the distinctions between locally experienced and abstractly imagined social bodies as well as the political subjectivities that are conventionally associated with them. The messy entanglement of the crowd and the masses becomes still more knotty in West's ambivalent politics. This ambivalence is especially striking in *A Cool Million* (1934) and *The Day of the Locust*, in which crowds are easily manipulated into fascism and violence at the same time that they mark opportunities for democratic organization. West's crowds are unique, however, in their defiance of readers' expectations of a smoothly uniform body, posing instead a distributed form, similar to the crowd, discussed in the introduction, in the final scene of Henry Roth's *Call It Sleep*. Instead of a homogenized social body, West emphasizes the diversity of the crowd's actors and their interests, as well as the friction and interpenetration of its constituents. Reading West's crowds as networked bodies helps readers bypass the typical political binary of the crowd, framed as either a revolutionary force of democratization or a repulsive manifestation of the vulgar and the so-called unwashed. This is particularly useful in West's case, given that this binary may be fundamentally irresolvable in his fiction. Instead, emphasizing the distributed nature of West's crowds allows readers to focus not on the crowds' content but their form. This device of network aesthetics proves useful to West and other moderns in responding to stressors of both local community and national space, as the conflation of crowd and the masses demonstrates, as well as in their responses to the crises in democracy itself.

West's crowds chart major discontinuities in network aesthetics. On the one hand, they might be read as yet another site negotiating the cultural logic of modernism—confronting massification, often within its metonymic setting of Hollywood, with the crowd as a figure of distribution. On the other hand, the political ambivalence of West's crowds signals a turn away from the utopian zeal for social distribution embraced by earlier network aesthetics. By identifying the crowd as a critical figure of distribution, West's fiction signals the decline of modern network aesthetics. Because the crowd is such an indelibly modern experience, it marks this device of network aesthetics as inextricably modern in equal measure and thereby limits later uses of the crowd. Indeed, in the postmodern contraction of network aesthetics to the six-degrees theory and hypertextual fiction, crowds such as West's are nowhere to be seen. This terminal point of modern network aesthetics, then, also haunts today's aesthetic experiments, which are either unable or unwilling to imagine connectivity alongside collectivity.

Crowds, Masses, Massification

West's interest in crowds and the masses appears throughout his works, demonstrating a sustained investment in new modes of social organization that were just appearing during—and do not seem to have survived—the modern period. His Hollywood novel, *The Day of the Locust*, is best known for its apocalyptic climax, in which a crowd converges at a movie premiere and ultimately turns to riot as "a crusading mob" (201). The scene brings to life protagonist Tod Hackett's long-planned painting "The Burning of Los Angeles" with all the terror and fury he imagined: it is "a great bonfire of architectural styles" with "the mob carrying baseball bats and torches" in the foreground, approaching the viewer (200–01). His earlier and lesser-known novella, *A Cool Million*, also concludes with a crowd scene, in which the "Pitkin Day" parade in honor of the novel's fallen protagonist Lemuel Pitkin draws crowds that clearly parody fascist mobilization. Crowds are also implied in West's novel of massification, *Miss Lonelyhearts* (1933), which follows a male advice columnist who acts as something of a confessor to the masses whom he cannot imagine as individuals. Lonelyhearts, derided by his editor as one of "the priests of twentieth-century America," attributes his letter writers' suffering to the culture industry (4). "Men have always fought their misery with dreams," he thinks. "Although dreams were once powerful, they have been made puerile by the movies, radio and newspapers. Among many betrayals, this one was the worst" (39). The "betrayals" of massification in this early work would return to motivate the climactic riot of *The Day of the Locust*.

West's unparalleled investment in the crowd and the masses—and its role in the closure of modern network aesthetics—is only understood in light of the uniquely modern experiences and discourses of crowds, the masses, and massification. Unlike the heralded features of the moderns' social landscape, this nexus of crowd and masses is poorly understood and warrants review. In "Haunted by Mass Culture" (2000), Susan Hegeman argues that the masses and their entertainments mark "a different arrangement of social space than the one we now experience" (300). Indeed, modern Americans experienced amusement parks, baseball parks, and, of course, movie palaces as inextricably public, crowded spaces. These spaces and others gave rise to spontaneous gatherings. In *The Great Crash, 1929* (1972), John Kenneth Galbraith, the Keynesian economist and advisor to Presidents Roosevelt, Kennedy, and Johnson, details the crowds gathering outside the New York Stock Exchange on Black Thursday—a setting to rival the apocalyptic conclusion of *The Day of the Locust*. The crowd formed at first because of a failure in network technology: the stock tickers had fallen hours behind because of the volume of trading, creating uncertainty as to just how badly the market was crashing. Galbraith details "a weird roar" that could be heard outside the Stock Exchange as a crowd gathered there (104). In Galbraith's telling, the crowd outside was less and less cognizant of the unfolding drama in the stock market. No one seemed to know what they were gathering for. When a workman appeared on a rooftop, the crowd fixated on him, assuming he was preparing to jump to his death and waiting rather impatiently for him to do so.[1] Variations on this scene were repeated across the country, with crowds forming outside branch offices and brokerage firms, being fed reports from ticker displays along with rumors and speculation (104–05). The ominous "weird roar" and the observers' increasing uncertainty about what they were gathering for must have made for a great deal of concern on the ground. What were these people gathering to do? Was it information they were after? Or rubbernecking? Or was riot on their minds? I emphasize Galbraith's story not to underscore the violent menace of the crowd but rather its spontaneity. Crowds during the modern period could come and go without any coordination whatsoever—a stark contrast to public gatherings today, and a tendency that, for many observers, gave the crowd a charge of dreadful unpredictability.

For West, this generalized milieu was rooted first and foremost in Hollywood. In his treatment of the culture industries' massification of social space, West takes up the concerns undergirding Randolph Bourne's "Trans-National America," the moderns' surrogate manifesto of network aesthetics. As chapter 1 has shown, Bourne's innovation of networked social organization responded largely to the prewar discourses of Americanism and cultural pluralism. Massified culture, however, also influences Bourne's distributed social space. Bourne laments mass culture's role in assimilation, warning that immigrants would adopt "the American culture of the cheap newspaper, the 'movies,' the popular song, the ubiquitous automobile" (113). An Americanism predicated on massification, Bourne warns, would lead to "the cultural wreckage of our time" (114). Working for the studios, and as a first-generation American born to Lithuanian immigrants, West lived the very situation that troubled Bourne.

Rather than submitting to this "wreckage," however, West shared Bourne's suspicion of mass culture. This position, as Rita Barnard notes in *The Great Depression and the Culture of Abundance* (1995), preoccupies West criticism of the late modern period, in which the general thrust depends on the now dated critical binaries of high and mass culture.[2] Though its only mention of West is a passing reference to a "mawkish travesty" of an adaptation of *Miss Lonelyhearts,* Dwight Macdonald's "Masscult and Midcult" is symptomatic of West's late modern critics. Macdonald's long history of masscult demonstrates the conventional late modern dichotomy of authenticity and commodity. "The post-1750 public, lacking the taste and knowledge of the old patron class, is not only satisfied with shoddy mass-produced goods but in general feels more at home with them," Macdonald writes (26). Like Bourne, West certainly found such aesthetics cheap—"a surfeit of shoddy" as Israel Satinpenny puts it in *A Cool Million* (217). And he understood his rare opportunities to write for the studios as no more than hackwork, as the steady reproduction of formulas.[3] Indeed, it is not a stretch to see West as readymade for Macdonald's lament of "the lumpen-avant-garde" and his jeremiad on the lack of an authentic high culture (55).

But the late modern reading of West mistakenly assumes that a critique of mass culture necessarily hinges on its production of degraded, homogeneized aesthetics. The isolation of aesthetics diminishes the other concern lurking behind the critique of massification: its homogenization of social organization. Macdonald's argument that people in a mass society "are related not to each other but to some abstract organizing principle" (23) is also attuned to this problem, particularly as it informed Bourne's transnationalism thesis. Of massification's negation of a knowable community, Macdonald concludes that mass culture renders cultural pluralism—or more precisely, Bourne's distributed transnationalism—an impossible goal (34). Macdonald thus exposes the broader social critique that underlies late modern aesthetic criticism.

Macdonald is also helpful in illuminating the perceived link between the masses and the crowd. A mass society forms its community by external referents, not by ties between its individuals, he writes, and the same is true of a crowd: "A mass society, like a crowd, is inchoate and uncreative. Its atoms cohere not according to individual liking or traditions or even interests, but in a purely mechanical way, as iron filings of different shapes and sizes are pulled toward a magnet working on the one quality they have in common" (9). A true community, by contrast, is a group of individuals who share common, concrete interests (8).[4] In Macdonald's formulation, both the masses and the crowd move in tandem toward an externalized homogenization, differing only in scale.

West's crowds provide more nuance in their distributed form, but Macdonald's framework signals the entrenched ideological positions that are entailed in discussions of the crowd. Such ideological entrenchment is exemplified by Gustave Le Bon, the French sociologist and social psychologist who, as noted in the introduction, proclaimed that the new century would usher in an "era of crowds."[5] Le Bon's diagnosis of the crowded century advanced two foundational fallacies of the crowd, its makeup, and its relationship to society that have proven so influential that his work is still being undone today. First, Le Bon posits the crowd as a completely monolithic, uniform body, in which individuals yield their own consciousness to the fused consciousness of the crowd. "The sentiments and ideas of all the persons in the gathering take one and the same direction," he writes, "and their conscious personality vanishes. A collective mind is formed, doubtless transitory, but presenting very clearly defined characteristics" (23–24). Le Bon's discussion of mob mentality draws heavily on late-nineteenth century scientific racism.[6] Second, Le Bon subscribes to a pernicious conflation of crowds and the masses that hinges on assumptions of class barbarism and violence—a conflation that others would extrapolate to the relationship between the crowd and the emergent mass culture. Le Bon opines: "Crowds are only powerful for destruction. Their rule is always tantamount to a barbarian phase. A civilisation involves fixed rules, discipline, a passing from the instinctive to the rational state, forethought for the future, an elevated degree of culture. . . . When the structure of a civilisation is rotten, it is always the masses that bring about its downfall" (18). The crowd's irreducible homogeneity, its innate nature of violence, and the slippage of these qualities to the larger and abstracted social body of the masses—these are the crowd discourses that West inherited, simultaneously writing within and against them.

Le Bon's reactionary attitudes toward crowds and masses underscore their novelty in the modern period. But although his writing may color some readers' reception of the crowd scenes in *A Cool Million* and *The Day of the Locust*, these texts do not fully adhere to Le Bon's formulations. Although both works flirt with Le Bon's presumptions of race- and class-based constituencies of the crowd, they also defy association with Le Bon's theories of the crowd's homogeneity and its direct equation with the masses. Instead, West's crowds are distributed and thereby suggest social formations that would flatten the very same institutional barriers such as class and ethnicity that prevail in Le Bon's understanding of crowds. These works do not track a perfect continuity, however. *A Cool Million* insists on the malevolence of the crowd and its proclivity for political manipulation—key components of West's parody of fascism. Indeed, in this earlier work the crowd is only called into being by the project of fascism. By situating the crowd into the literal and figurative settings of Hollywood, *The Day of the Locust* instead positions the crowd in the broader experience of mass culture. Taken together, these narratives assert the distribution of the crowd against massification, one of the signal polarities of the cultural logic of modernism.

Cool Crowds: Democratic Form, Fascist Content

A Cool Million is what Michael Denning pithily refers to as an "inverted Horatio Alger tale" (*Cultural Front* 244). Indeed, as Douglas Shepard and Gary Scharnhorst have shown, West's homage to Alger borders on outright plagiarism, mimicking not only character and plot sequences but also closely replicating entire sentences and paragraphs.[7] On his quest to make millions, young Lemuel meets setback after setback, each leaving him further from material gain than before. He is ripped off by con men several times; a case of mistaken identity lands him in jail and further depletes his wealth; he is pressed into service as a homosexual sex slave, which results in his arrest, a shakedown by a public attorney, a plea deal, and his release to the streets, penniless. And these financial calamities reflect the bodily deformations he endures along the way: the removal of his teeth, the loss of an eye, the amputations of a thumb and a leg, and even a scalping. For every step Lemuel takes toward the American dream of wealth and leisure, he seems to take several more back to poverty and infirmity. In its appropriation and negation of Alger's bootstraps myth,

A Cool Million is a tale of the delusion of the American masses by the impossible, mythical success narrative. And this rendering of the abstract masses is but a part of the text's valences of the crowd and the masses.

Alongside its critique of their ideological manipulation by the Alger narrative, *A Cool Million* also shows a more expressly political manipulation of the American masses as they are duped into fascism. The crowd, a staple figure for fascism's seduction of the masses, asserts its central role in West's narrative. As he sinks into the underworld of crime and extreme poverty, Lemuel becomes acquainted with a distinctly fascist impulse circulating among the breadlines of the Depression. Nathan "Shagpoke" Whipple, the former president from Lemuel's hometown whom Rita Barnard describes as "a Calvin Coolidge turned fascist" (149), first sends Lemuel out into the world on grandiose promises of American opportunity. Lemuel meets him again years later after Whipple has fallen on hard times, as he stands outside a Salvation Army canteen drumming up support for his new organization: "the National Revolutionary Party, popularly known as the 'Leather Shirts'" (172). Whipple espouses a populism that is an unmistakable parody of fascism, and it is no accident that the bulk of the scenes addressing this parody center on two crowd gatherings—each of which demonstrates the manipulation and mobilization of crowd and masses in the march toward fascism.

The first crowd demonstrates Whipple's ability to influence a strictly delimited group of people. Working for a traveling freak show that doubles as a communist propaganda organ, Whipple finds an opportunity to advance the Leather Shirts campaign at a stop in the South. He exhorts a crowd of white men to rebel against the propagandizing leader of the traveling show and is met with a disproportionately violent response as the crowd disperses, "shouting 'Lynch him! Lynch him!' although a good three-quarters of its members did not know whom it was they were supposed to lynch" (228). The crowd's violence then spreads in a grisly comedy of errors: "Another section of Shagpoke's audience, made up mostly of older men, had somehow gotten the impression that the South had again seceded from the Union. . . . They ran up the Confederate flag on the courthouse pole, and prepared to die in its defense" (229). The crowd's violence becomes a full-blown riot in which African Americans' heads are paraded on poles, a Jew is nailed to a door, and a Catholic priest's housekeeper is raped. The passage clearly parodies the stereotypes of Southern racism, anti-Semitism, and anti-Catholicism, and it also suggests the easy manipulation of a crowd. The ease with which the crowd fragments into these sects suggests that they were always there—that it is not a breakdown of a coherent unit that is at work but the revelation of the factions that were already inside it.

But Whipple would not be deterred by this failed attempt to realize his fascist vision. The novel concludes with a second crowd scene that features Whipple's ability to lead the entire nation to fascism, the crowd of the novel's final sequence standing in for the masses of the United States. After Lemuel is made an involuntary martyr for the Leather Shirts cause, West gives us something of an afterword in the account of the Pitkin's Birthday celebration, a prolepsis that marks the ascendancy of Whipple's new political regime. Whipple presides over a parade commemorating Lemuel as propaganda for the National Revolutionary Party. The parade is, of course, a fitting setting for this politically tinged crowd. Orson Welles, obsessed by the intersections of politics and aesthetics in fascism during his Popular Front years, would observe: "Showmanship is fundamental to the fascist strategy, and the chief fascist argument is the parade" (Denning, *Cultural Front* 365).[8] West's crowd accompanies such a parade through New York: "It is Pitkin's Birthday, a national holiday, and the youth of America is parading down Fifth Avenue in his honor. They are a hundred thousand strong. On every boy's head is a coonskin hat complete with jaunty tail, and on every shoulder rests a squirrel rifle" (*Cool Million* 237). When the parade reaches the reviewing stand, Whipple addresses the youths, casting Lemuel as an icon of the party's xenophobic tenets. The crowd observing Pitkin's Birthday is overpowered by Whipple's distortions of Lemuel's biography, and the novel concludes with their dissonant exclamations: "'Hail the Martyrdom in the Bijou Theatre!,' 'Hail, Lemuel Pitkin!,' and 'All hail, the American Boy!'" (238). Though it comes as little solace given the mass deception that completes the rise of fascist rule, this dissonance demonstrates the stubborn heterogeneity of the crowd, much like the factions within the crowd of Southern whites.

In both the Southerners' lynch mob and the Pitkin's Birthday parade, the crowds' manipulability resonates with Le Bon's thesis that spontaneous formations are controlled by a mechanism akin to hypnosis. The crowd operates, he writes, "in a special state, which much resembles the state of fascination in which the hypnotized individual finds himself in the hands of the hypnotiser. . . . The conscious personality has entirely vanished; will and discernment are lost"

(31). And this hypnosis signals not only the manipulation but the homogeneity of the crowd as a fused unit, as the entire crowd is hypnotized into a shared psychological state.[9] Read this way, the crowd can only confirm the moderns' misgivings about the hypnotic delusions of fascism. But while Whipple's role as skillful manipulator of crowds smacks of the hypnotist, it is wrong to say, as Le Bon might, that the crowds are uniform in their state of agitation. Instead, West provides clear evidence that these crowds, even while they are manipulated as a discrete group, demonstrate internal variability. After Whipple's inflammatory speech to the Southern whites, the crowd separates into three factions: the first heads to the opera house that staged the freak show, the second heads to defend the Confederate flag on the courthouse flagpole, and the third proceeds to the town's principal stores and to free their relatives from jail. The diversification of that crowd, alongside the very dissonance of the crowd's cries at the Pitkin's Birthday parade, demonstrates that even while a spontaneous body can be manipulated as a single organism—toward violence, toward fascism, and so on—it still retains a distinctly distributed composition. That these crowds maintain internal diversification may seem like a commonplace, but it is important to recognize how West's crowds preserve that networked organization precisely against Le Bon's pervasive theories that treated the crowd as a homogeneous unit. It is this distribution that gives the crowd its truly modern quality.

The networked diversification of these crowds also challenges the assumption that West's crowds are simply fascist. Rather than simply reading them as monolithic and interchangeable units doing Whipple's bidding, an emphasis on the distributed composition of these two crowds allows readers to see how the networked constitution of crowds actually disrupts their manipulability. In the case of the Southerners, the crowd's factionalism undermines West's portrayal of the crowd as the puppet to Whipple's puppeteer. And the dissonance of the crowd at the parade signals that the crowd cannot be shoehorned into perfect orthodoxy, leaving room—or at least hope—for an alternative to Whipple's ideological regime. Although it is easy enough for Whipple to stir up the animosities of these crowds, it is another thing entirely for him to direct them into concerted action. Their interests and energies are too diverse to be controlled. Perversely, the diverse interests of the groups—which political, ethnic, or religious group shall the Southerners persecute? and how best to celebrate the fascist hero Pitkin?—signal a democratic form to these crowds despite their appearing fascist in content.

Recognizing the tensions within Whipple's crowds—fascist content straining against democratic, distributed form—allows readers to bypass the traditional readings of fascism's grip on crowds and on the masses and instead foregrounds the possibilities of resistance posed by these networked bodies. By virtue of its work with crowds, *The Day of the Locust* is often read as having a similar engagement with fascism—though at an allegorical remove, given the absence of politicians or political rallies such as those of the earlier text. It is the direct treatment of an objectionable political platform that makes *A Cool Million* helpful in illuminating the meaning of crowds in *The Day of the Locust*. By straining against such an obviously insupportable project as fascism, the crowds of the former text allow readers to see a more generalizable resistance performed by the crowds of *The Day of the Locust*—a resistance situated within the tensions of the cultural logic of modernism.

Of and against Massification: Crowds and Democracy in *The Day of the Locust*

Unlike Whipple's crowds in *A Cool Million*, *The Day of the Locust*'s riotous climax and its other crowd scenes have no explicit political motivation. What they have in common—and what distinguishes them from their counterparts in West's earlier fiction—is their situation in the Hollywood novel genre. By the time *The Day of the Locust* was published, most of the conventions of the genre were well established—tropes of the promised land of glitzy opportunities, the fallen woman who fails at acting and turns to sex work, and so on. As John Parris Springer observes in *Hollywood Fictions* (2000), "fiction about movie making first appeared in the early teens as juvenile literature" (8), and by the 1930s it was an easily recognizable genre, with *The Day of the Locust* having been preceded by James M. Cain's *The Postman Always Rings Twice* (1934), McCoy's *They Shoot Horses, Don't They?* (1935), Richard Hallas's *You Play the Black and the Red Comes Up* (1938), and John O'Hara's *Hope of Heaven* (1938). For West, the Hollywood novel held a strong appeal, given his fraught relationship with the studios and his longstanding interests in surrealist epistemologies. West's contribution to this generic tradition lies in his use of the crowd. On the one hand, the crowds in Hollywood are the product of the culture industries—a conventional association for West's contemporaries and for scholarship today. On the other hand, the crowds of *The Day of the Locust* are highly resistant to

Hollywood's massification of social space. Whereas *A Cool Million*'s crowds act as simultaneously a product of and a bulwark against fascism's narrowly defined political project, the same social formations in *The Day of the Locust* now mediate the universal tensions of modern experience.

That West's Hollywood novel would invest itself so thoroughly in the representation of crowds should come as no surprise, for movie theaters were one of the primary sites associated with the crowd—and especially anxiety over the power of the crowd—during the early 1900s. With the advent of moving-picture projectors in the 1890s, the nickelodeon theater emerged as a space typified by rowdiness and crowdedness that was inseparable from its working-class, immigrant patronage. Accordingly, the nickelodeon was a major locus of intellectual output, not only over the products of popular culture consumed there, but also for the crowds drawn to the theaters—their democratizing potential, their potential for societal corruption, and so on. The nickelodeon was so deeply associated with the crowd, Russ Castronovo writes in *Beautiful Democracy* (2007), that in 1915 "the film industry began encouraging patrons to speak not of 'movies' but of the more respectable-sounding 'photoplays' in an effort to help cinema shed its dodgy background of immigrant and working-class contexts" (138). Despite this bid for respectability, Castronovo argues, the early movie audiences were conceived not as singular spectators but as crowds. In Castronovo's reading, crowds defined not only Hollywood's audience and a great deal of the content of its films but were in fact manufactured by Hollywood's culture industry.[10] That the crowd itself was an object of the culture industry's production was readily recognized during the earliest days of film, and the sublime awe and fear of this phenomenon lies at the heart of *The Day of the Locust*.

West places the crowds of *The Day of the Locust* in his own present, well after the decline of the nickelodeon era. Though the residual association between film and the immigrant crowd remained even in the late 1930s, by this time the industry's transition to the "movie palace" made film a much more widely consumed commodity. In *The Cultural Front*, Denning estimates that movies accounted for three-quarters of Americans' leisure spending by 1937 (41). Rita Barnard adds that during this period Works Progress Administration unemployment funds, in guidelines for both the household "emergency budget" and the "maintenance budget," had "specifically allotted funds to enable each family member to attend the movies: once a month on the former, and once a week on the latter," fueling the rise of the film industry as well as the American ideology of consumption (25). So at the publication of *The Day of the Locust*, the movie theater occupied a dual space regarding the crowd and the masses. On the one hand, it still bore the residual association with the nickelodeon's urban, immigrant, working-class crowd. On the other hand, the movie theater had become the locus of a truly massified consumer society, severed from its formerly urban locale and its associations of class and ethnicity to begin to saturate the entire nation.

The Day of the Locust renders the entanglement of these two figures—the crowd of the nickelodeon era and the masses produced by and consuming the culture industries—and their mediation by modern massification. This dynamic begins well before the apocalyptic crowd scene that concludes the novel. The introductory passage, in which Tod Hackett observes the studio backlot scene of extras marching toward their set, pales in comparison to the climactic finale, but it establishes some of the intersections of the crowd, the masses, and mass media. Alongside the famous finale, this passage effectively frames *The Day of the Locust* between bookends of crowd scenes. Hackett looks out over his set and costume design materials to see an army passing below his window. It is the usual backlot conceit: the narration fools the reader into believing something truly momentous is happening only to reveal that the event was merely the stuff of a Hollywood production. The telling detail, however, lies in how West's narrator describes the cast and crew as they pass by: "An army of cavalry and foot was passing. It moved like a mob; its lines broken, as though fleeing some terrible defeat" (21). The army parade's descent into an unregimented mob indicates the falsehood of the Hollywood representation of military regimentation, as if reflecting the massification of film itself. It also suggests the very audience of such a cultural commodity, which is simultaneously commodified as a product of the film industry and is reified as a figure of the masses. In other words, the simile likening the army of cast and crew to a mob evokes the specter of the nickelodeon's bygone raucous crowds.

Such a nickelodeon audience manifests almost literally in the crowd that gathers to watch a stag film at Mrs. Jenning's upscale call house. Migrating over from the fashionable party at Claude Estee's house, Tod and the industry insiders sit down for a screening of *Le Predicament de Marie, ou La Bonne Distraite*—a piece about an oversexed family and its maid that sets up a correspondingly oversexed scene in the theater. Even as the projectionist is preparing to start the film, the crowd of moviegoers is boisterous: "Mrs. Schwartzen started to whistle and stamp her feet and the others joined in. They imitated a rowdy audience in the days of the nickelodeon" (44). This boisterousness only builds in correspondence with the sexual tension in the film until the film projector breaks down and ruins any hope of a climactic payoff for the family or for Tod's crew of spectators. West literalizes the aesthete's lament that massified culture poses a vulgar and ultimately unfulfilling appeal to libidinal satisfaction.

But the rowdiness at the screening is more than a performance or another sign of the Estee cohort's Hollywood affect. Rather, it muddles the classed nature of crowds across the text. In *Around Quitting Time* (2001), Robert Seguin observes the moment when Mrs. Jenning's film projector breaks down, leading the crowd into unrest: "'It's a frameup,' someone yelled. 'Fake!' 'Cheat!' 'The old teaser routine!' They stamped their feet and whistled" in what West describes as a "mock riot" (*Locust* 45–46). "This reminds us once more of *The Cheated*, the original title of the book," Seguin notes, "and establishes the fact that we are at some level not to understand these high-living Hollywood socialites as distinct from the scrambling lumpens who populate the rest of the novel, that some deeper fictional identity unites them" (104). Indeed, the novel's title suggests this class ambivalence. The draft that Random House first accepted was entitled "The Cheated," but in intervening drafts West also considered "The Grass Eaters," "Cry Wolf," and "The Wrath to Come" as viable contenders for the title. Martin reads "The Grass Eaters" as signaling enmity toward the crowd, and other titles could be understood similarly—"Cry Wolf" underscoring the manipulability of the masses and "The Wrath to Come" foretelling violence and barbarism befitting Le Bon's pernicious assumptions about the working class. As these readings go, the working titles and even the final title charge the working class with mass psychosis. But it is crucial to state that these readings are only projections of Le Bon's frameworks of the crowd's monolithic uniformity and racially derived barbarism. Seguin points readers in another direction, offering an alternative understanding of the crowd and the masses. For Seguin, Mrs. Jenning provides a setting in which class hierarchy is flattened in the elite's relation to what Macdonald calls "the lumpen-avant-garde." Unlike the settings of *Gentlemen Prefer Blondes*, where this flattening takes place when characters from an array of class positions come into direct contact, West's flattening takes place only in the mediation of mass culture, and it only becomes visible in the crowd.

The "deeper fictional identity" Seguin detects across the novel's various class positions is made clear in a repetition of the term "cheated" in the text's climactic scene outside Kahn's Persian Palace Theatre. Now, instead of the Hollywood insiders and the other elite of Claude Estee's circle, the crowd is made up of thousands of ordinary people hoping to glimpse celebrities at the premier. The narrator reflects on the crowd before it is sparked to violence: "Nothing can ever be violent enough to make taut their slack minds and bodies. They have been cheated and betrayed. They have slaved and saved for nothing" (193). "Cheated and betrayed" again, just as with the betrayals of *Miss Lonelyhearts*—the text lays bare the nature of the betrayal of all those who, as Tod says, had "come to California to die": "They realize that they've been tricked and burn with resentment. Every day of their lives they read the newspapers and went to the movies. Both fed them on lynchings, murder, sex crimes, explosions, wrecks, love nests, fires, miracles, revolutions, wars. This daily diet made sophisticates of them" (23, 192). Fused by the mass media, the crowd and the masses share a common betrayal—the moderns' conventional lament of the culture industries. The repetition of "cheated" to describe both elite and ordinary people demonstrates the totalizing function of mass culture, which extends beyond Le Bon's frameworks of class and ethnicity to suggest a complete massification of the United States' social space.

Indeed, the assembly outside Kahn's—described in turn as a "crowd," a "mob," and finally a "riot"—demonstrates this flattening with its internal makeup. Seguin corrects the traditional readings that the text's final crowd is strictly a working-class or lower-middle-class phenomenon. On the one hand, West offers an unequivocal statement of the crowd's makeup: "Tod could see very few people who looked tough, nor could he see any working men. The crowd was made up of the lower middle class, every other person one of his torchbearers" (191). On the other hand, he allows for a wide variety of daily working experiences that broaden the crowd's class spectrum, if inadvertently: "All their lives they had slaved at some kind of dull, heavy labor, behind desks and counters, in the fields and at tedious machines of all sorts" (192). It seems as if West is trying to have it both ways, labeling the crowd "lower middle class"—not coincidentally the class most often associated with fascism—in one moment and describing it as composed of a range of white- and blue-collar workers the next. Of this shift, Seguin argues that the crowd is considerably more diverse than one might expect at first glance (111). The crowd, then, rebukes each of Le Bon's fundamental premises, presenting an internally differentiated social body instead of a homogeneous one and eschewing the crowd's raced and classed connotations. Whether at Mrs. Jenning's or outside Kahn's theater, in other words, the crowd and mass culture are capable of transcending the class binaries that motivate John Dos Passos's *U.S.A.* trilogy in its lamentation "all right we are two nations" and that have provided a stubborn resistance to the projects of modern network aesthetics.

West does not stage the masses as having an inherent inclination toward violence, as Le Bon argued. Instead, the crowd outside Kahn's is an inert social body that remains placid until violence calls it into violence. Nevertheless, the conventional bias against the crowd is evident at the earliest moment Tod sees it. The narrator describes his observation of the policemen trying to keep the roads open for traffic: "He noticed how worried they looked and how careful they tried to be. If they had to arrest someone, they joked good-naturedly with the culprit, making light of it until they got him around the corner, then they whaled him with their clubs" (190). Tod himself registers a portentous feeling about the crowd, thinking: "At the sight of their heroes and heroines, the crowd would turn demoniac. Some little gesture, either too pleasing or too offensive, would start it moving and then nothing but machine guns would stop it. Individually the purpose of its members might simply be to get a souvenir, but collectively it would grab and rend" (190). Although intense anxiety surrounds the formation of the crowd, the crowd itself is docile. It causes the police some logistical problems, periodically bulging out into the streets, and it is loud with the "continuous roar of catcalls, laughter and yells, pierced occasionally by a scream" (190). Never, however, does the crowd demonstrate a potential for anything more than unruliness. The anxieties demonstrated by the police, Tod, and a reporter covering the premier are wholly out of step with the reality of the crowd's mundane nature, and they only receive post hoc justification after the crowd is set into tumult by the beating of the child actor Adore Loomis at the hands of Homer Simpson, the dull Midwesterner who comes to California to bask in the sun. That this is the event setting the crowd into motion is telling. Although the crowd does not act collectively to redress Simpson's brutal attack and even devolves into its own state of depravity in its numerous sexual assaults, it is only induced to violence by Homer's act of violence. The crowd is rendered as a mirror or as a vessel, only reflecting the qualities cast onto it or into it, and the result is a refusal to present the crowd as inherently malevolent.

The violence that ultimately breaks out overshadows for many readers the democratic politics the crowd carries in its formal composition. On the surface, the crowd appears monolithic in its violent surge, bearing a strong likeness to Le Bon's uniform, hive-minded collective. For instance, Tod, caught in the melee, experiences the crowd as a rather homogeneous body of water: "He was jostled about in a hacking cross surf of shoulders and backs. . . . Using the eucalyptus tree as a landmark, he tried to work toward it by slipping sideways against the tide, pushing hard when carried away from it and riding the current when it moved toward his objective" (196–97). Inside the lurching mass of people, however, Tod begins to recognize different divisions within the crowd. One segment spasms with the jostling of bodies, with men grabbing after the torn dress of a young girl. Another segment is so placid that "most of the people seemed to be enjoying themselves" while they analyze the antics of their more animated counterparts and discuss how the riot was initiated in the first place (198). And even within that segment, Tod encounters individuals in some profile, bringing into relief the nodal constitution of the crowd. Tod sees Homer's "head bobbing above the crowd" before he beats Adore Loomis (193). In the violent segment of the crowd, Tod can see the anonymous young girl whom he chivalrously protects from an old man's sexual assault, only to find a second man grabbing at her body and torn dress. In a docile segment of the crowd, he is able to eavesdrop on the conversation between a "stout woman," her male companion, a woman at her side, "a little man wearing a cloth cap," and a third woman (199). This segmentation into separate modes of being within the crowd and into individuals establishes the distribution of West's crowd, supplanting its monolithic façade with an internal structure akin to a constellation.

The crowd's distributed form stands in stark contrast to the massified social space posed by the very culture industry it has gathered to venerate. Indeed, the paradox of the crowd at the movie premiere is that its form resists the totalizing, hegemonic tendency of mass culture. In this way, it not only defies Le Bon's ideologies of this group formation's social politics. Rather, it negotiates mass culture as an agent of the cultural logic of modernism—the pull of homogeneity against dispersal, totality against the fragment. West adopts Bourne's critique of massified social space, as well as some of its major points of origin, "the American culture of the cheap newspaper, the 'movies,' the popular song, the ubiquitous automobile." This is also Macdonald's social-aesthetic critique of "the lumpen-avant-garde." But whereas Bourne and Macdonald relegate this massification to the lower orders of the United States' class strata, West shows its full saturation of the elite and workers alike. The novel's completion of the project of massification would confirm Macdonald's worst fears: that even the vanguard curators of culture are corrupted and untrustworthy and that masscult negates the possibility of community by directing individuals' relations not to each other but to an external and abstract mediator. *The Day of the Locust*'s crowds, however, mark a final resistance to massification—a compromised resistance, perhaps, but nevertheless a repudiation of the rhetorical conflation of crowd, masses, and massification.

Even in *The Day of the Locust,* however, West's fiction retains a twofold note of ambivalence on the crowd—a cautiousness that should inform our understanding of modern network aesthetics and the harsh social conditions of their moment and ours. At times, the networked body of the crowd seems on the verge of imploding or dissolving into an undifferentiated mass, as if the figure has reached the end of its usefulness or West simply prefers a completely massified form as the method of subverting mass culture. And this ambivalence is related to another that concerns the crowd's relation to class. For although his crowds' unruliness defies manipulation and their distributed qualities transcend class binaries, the matter of class stratification remains elusive in West's fiction. For instance, in the penultimate draft of *Locust,* West provided a much more dramatic outcome for the riot at the novel's climax. Martin writes that this draft included a middle-class Angeleno element that would radicalize in southern California and spread across the nation. "Only the working classes would resist," West writes in this draft. "There would be civil war" (Martin 319). Instead of imploding into a fused mass, the crowd gives way to the striations of class rank. West ultimately withdrew the middle-class figures, as well as the direct language of class antagonism, but its traces are still evident in the novel. Does this sedimentary draft signal sympathy for a revolution led by "the cheated"? Or horror at their barbaric potential? And why does the networked form of the crowd give way to class striation? It is hard indeed to disentangle such questions from the classed discourses of the crowd that date back to Le Bon.

In any case, the messy valences of crowds and class in West's fiction underscore the degree to which class has proven a stubborn obstacle not only to the reorganization but especially to the imaginary of national and social space.

In other words, the reassertion of class identity in *Locust*'s penultimate draft suggests that class consciousness is perhaps as durable as class structure. And as with the *U.S.A.* trilogy's "two nations" thesis of an insuperable class binary, the persistent ambivalence of class in West's fiction signals the challenge of modern network aesthetics to transcend class and produce collectivity out of its connectivity. As previous chapters have discussed, the clash between the network and this binary formation exposes one of the signal conditions of the modern period: income disparity widened and hardened during the 1920s to further polarize class stratification, and of course its effects were felt still more immediately during the Depression era. This gap is such a naturalized feature of American social geography that it has only very recently become speakable in public policy discussions. Yet even while this widened class gulf defines our present in the United States and across the globe—it is, after all, the inevitable consequence of capitalism and perhaps even its endgame—there are major discontinuities between our network aesthetics and those of the moderns, and they become visible in West's fiction, ambivalent as it is.

One virtue of West's messy class politics is that, in posing the crowd against class hierarchy, against fascism, and against a broader range of massification, West's novels bring modern network aesthetics to bear on democracy. This is not an aberrant application. For Le Bon, democracy was one of the major stakes of the crowd, and indeed this pairing continues to be scrutinized in recent scholarship from Mary Esteve and Russ Castronovo. In the modern period, "democracy" still connoted, at least in part, an equality of condition. This understanding of democracy is mirrored in the distributed form of West's crowds, in which the people themselves do dual duty, acting as both the nodes to be connected as well as the mediating lines that constitute interconnection and draw the network. As such, West's crowds demonstrate a pure form of democracy, distributing all social identities into a flattened aggregate against atomistic dispersal and—especially in West's affiliation with the studios—total massification. Whereas Bourne might have located in these crowds his zeal for the Beloved Community, West regards them with some ambivalence, demonstrating a turn away from the utopian distributed space of earlier network aesthetics. Nevertheless, West's crowds heed the call from Bourne's surrogate manifesto of network aesthetics to "investigate what Americanism may rightly mean" after the failure of the massifying melting pot, providing the localized corollary of Bourne's transnationalism of the United States' social space ("Trans-National" 108).

On Closure

There is something paradoxical about identifying the schisms and the closure of modern network aesthetics. A schism negates the spatial dimension of a network by asserting disconnected, parallel structures instead of distribution. And closure defies the fundamental logic of networks, which operate on a principle of ever-expanding assimilation. How can a network be cleaved into a schism? How can it be contained by closure? These paradoxes are partly a consequence of arguing in the scholarly conventions of linearity, which allow or even encourage thinking about schisms and closures in ways that a work of network aesthetics might resist. But schisms and closure are nonetheless helpful in thinking about the distinctive qualities of modern network aesthetics—and especially their literary history, in which they are largely discontinuous with later aesthetic production. The schisms produced by Dos Passos's *U.S.A.* trilogy, as the preceding chapter discusses, facilitate a departure from high modern formal experimentation with network aesthetics and can be read as leading to West's ambivalence toward the utopian possibilities of distributed social space. Likewise, the period-specific nature of West's fiction forecloses altogether the moment of modern network aesthetics.

This closure is the result of hitching modern network aesthetics to the crowd, thereby rooting it in a device so inextricably modern as to be incompatible with—indeed, nearly unimaginable in—subsequent historical and social conditions. Both as a symbolic figure of social organization and as a lens of lived experience, the crowd marks a social space that seems to have expired with the passing of the modern period. Arguing that the modern period exhibited "a different arrangement of social space than the one we now experience," Hegeman points to the widespread experiences of mass culture and the public, both of which have precipitously declined since—and because of—the Cold War years. She surveys the 1934 sinking of the *Morro Castle* off the coast of Asbury Park, New Jersey, as an example of this phenomenon. As many as a quarter million people gathered to watch the ship slowly sink. The event drew sensationalist media coverage, which in turn attracted beachside vendors hawking souvenirs and prompted the state to reduce railway fares to spark further tourism. Hegeman characterizes the scene as "both a spontaneous public festival and a media event" ("Haunted" 298). The scene is reminiscent of Galbraith's crowds gathering spontaneously before the Stock

Exchange on Black Thursday, though of a completely different scale and duration. For Hegeman, this scene demonstrates precisely what so many of the mass culture critics feared: the people on the beach seemed manipulated by the press, the souvenir vendors catered to truly lurid tastes, and the tourism bureau demonstrated an unpleasant likeness to "insidious political forces of charismatic populism and totalitarianism" (299). The spectacle on the beach also demonstrates the remove we feel today from the possibilities of spontaneous formation, given the atomizing forces of suburbanization, home entertainment technologies, and the increasing privatization of public spaces that have become more and more prevalent since the midcentury.[11] "Though it is true that spontaneous public gatherings still appear at the sites of sensational murders or other gruesome events," Hegeman argues, "they seldom develop the carnivalesque air the *Morro Castle* provoked, precisely because we are now less familiar with the forms and norms of public entertainment in general" (300). Indeed, the 2013 Boston Marathon bombing demonstrates this shift in public space. After the bombings at the Marathon—itself a highly ritualized event that manages participants' and spectators' spontaneous impulses—Massachusetts governor Deval Patrick advised people to "stay out of crowds and calmly make their way home, or if they're visiting, back to their hotels" (Siegel and Block). Initial media reports emphasized the great role of bystanders in aiding the wounded, much like the climactic scene of Roth's *Call It Sleep*, but ultimately the "shelter-in-place" policy's atomization of public space defined the day.

The precipitousness of this decline leaves open powerful questions for scholars of modernisms. Hegeman attributes it to a shift from a largely urban and public culture to a more private one, noting, among other symptoms, the turn away from public entertainment ("Haunted" 300). In *The Crowd in American Literature* (1986), Nicolaus Mills offers another potential explanation in shifting economic conditions at the close of the Depression: between June 1940 and December 1941, the number of unemployed dropped from 8.5 to less than 4 million (112). This may well be one factor in the decline of the crowd, though of course unemployment or underemployment does not fully account for the modern zeitgeist and its differences from our own. Still more generally, this tidal shift registers as an effect—perhaps also as a cause—in the prevailing antagonism against the commons today, spurred by neoliberal ideologies of privatization and the decline of an ethos of the public. Whatever the manifold causes, the decline in such public and spontaneous gatherings—the waning of the crowd itself, in other words—marks a momentous, and generally underappreciated, development in twentieth-century American history. It follows that any aesthetic rendering of the crowd would be consigned to its historical moment. This is the unfortunate lot of West's crowds, which punctuate the end of modernism's investments in network aesthetics while also signaling the same fate for one of its trademark social formations. We still see crowds in contemporary narrative, of course, but usually as an object of setting rather than an agential body evocative of social organization. Indeed, in today's network aesthetics, where six-degrees-of-separation narratives and hypertextual fiction reign, the crowd escapes the imagination of distribution.

It is a curious occurrence, then, that critical theory takes up what narrative has relegated to modernist aesthetic production. Theory, in other words, marks a continuity with West's distributed crowds that contemporary narrative does not. For example, cued in part by Giorgio Agamben's theory of singularity, Michael Hardt and Antonio Negri position the multitude as a rhizomatic social formation of the commons that is arising in response to the striations of global capital. Throughout their *Empire* trilogy (2000–09), the multitude acts as a crowd figure for the era of globalization. In *Multitude* (2004), they describe it as an inherently distributed figure: "an open and expansive network in which all differences can be expressed freely and equally, a network that provides the means of encounter so that we can work and live in common" (xii–xiv). In *Commonwealth* (2009), they stress that this body is "not a spontaneous political subject but a project of political organization" (169). In other words, the multitude displays the distributed composition of the crowd, only it is globalized and organizes itself for political action. Other contemporary thinkers invoke the swarm as a corollary to the modern crowd. In *The Exploit*, for instance, Alexander R. Galloway and Eugene Thacker study the swarm as both demonstrating and being produced by a "tension that appears in the combination of formlessness and deliberate strategy, emergence and control, or amorphousness and coordination" (66). In their reading, the swarm is politically ambivalent, adopted for insurgency, civil disobedience, military strategy, and so on. If the crowd remains thinkable after all, why is this only so in the domain of theory? If massification, one of the formative conditions of the modern crowd, has only deepened since West's milieu, why has the figure diminished in contemporary narrative?

I ask these questions not to wax nostalgic about the modern milieu but to reflect on the nature of the cultural logic of modernism, manifested in the tensions between totality and fragment, centralization and dispersal. One way to understand the passing of this dialectic—or at least the moderns' particular inventions of network aesthetics that emerged to address it—would be to accept Jean-François Lyotard's pronouncement of the end of the grand narrative. In Lyotard's formulation, the fragment ascends over its former tension with totality, nullifying the cultural logic of modernism. This would explain the refusal of contemporary narrative to engage the kind of group dynamics posed by West's crowds, there being no imagination of the crowd or the commons in the age of the fragment. After all, even within the field of modern network aesthetics, West is something of an outlier in his use of a figure so closely associated with social homogeneity. Bourne, for example, emphasizes the ethnic enclave's autonomy, whereas West emphasizes the broader group, marking a shift in perspective from nodes and lines to the constellation itself that might augur the later shift away from the crowd and the masses. But to accept Lyotard's proposal that totalization—as a form of thought or a mode of social experience—is today inert would be to reject the bare facts of our pervasive mass media and of our defining experiences of globalization. If anything, the pull between fragment and totality has intensified since the modern period, marking continuity with the signal tensions of the modern period, if not exactly with the "different arrangement of social space" Hegeman identifies. This escalation is typified in the culture industry itself. On the one hand, our culture industries demonstrate a profound concentration of media ownership, which is consolidated into the control of some dozen firms including the Walt Disney Company, News Corp, and Time Warner. On the other hand, as Denning writes in *Culture in the Age of Three Worlds* (2004), these very same media conglomerates "look less like a mass culture and more like a series of elaborate, interlocking subcultures, each with their own market share" (102). These interlocking corporations of global capital bring to mind those of the American corporation that gave rise to network models during the modern period, as discussed in the introduction. This is to say that the cultural logic of modernism remains with us, though the full complement of the moderns' originary responses to it does not.

This paradox of historical continuity and aesthetic discontinuity has resulted in a major displacement: the visibly collective body of the crowd has been supplanted by the more abstractly connective group formations of the six-degrees narratives that prevail today. This displacement nullifies the initial impetus of network aesthetics, which, under Bourne's surrogate manifesto, derives from his quest for the Beloved Community. It was in pursuit of this ideal that Bourne imagined transnationalism as a means of salvaging American social space. "All our idealisms," Bourne concludes his manifesto, "must be those of future social goals in which all can participate, the good life of personality lived in the environment of the Beloved Community" ("Trans-National" 123). "It must be a future America," he continues, "on which all can unite, which pulls us irresistibly toward it, as we understand each other more warmly. To make real this striving amid dangers and apathies is a work for a younger *intelligentsia* of America" (123). West's crowds, ambivalent as they are, pose one answer to Bourne's challenge. Our field of network aesthetics today has yet to respond in kind.

Notes

Introduction

1. See, for instance, Janet Hobhouse's rehearsal of this anecdote in *Everybody Who Was Anybody* (1975), 68.

2. See also Diana Souhami's *Gertrude and Alice* (1991), 95.

3. Stein's formal project converges with her more widely discussed renovation of style. Richard Bridgman writes: "This early in her career [Stein] made no attempt to unify the style in revision. Rather she accepted the vagaries of her sensibility. The result was undeniably peculiar. The mixture of patches of normal prose, awkward locutions, cultivated eccentricities, and reflections of servant mentality produced a crazy quilt of style" (50). Patches and quilts—these are conventional metaphors that scholars use to contend with the central issue of this book, the moderns' interplay of fragment and totality.

4. For instance, in his seminal study *The Dialect of Modernism* (1994), Michael North situates "Melanctha" in the pan-Africanist discourses that informed Western modern invention from the turn of the century through the 1920s. He argues that Stein used the image of the African mask to address expatriation, lesbian desire, and the performativity of race and gender (66–75).

5. The bibliography of David Bordwell's "Mutual Friends and Chronologies of Chance" catalogues some 150 international films, mostly from the 1990s and 2000s, that follow this model. Salient examples include *Short Cuts* (1993), *71 Fragments* (1994), *Amores Perros* (2000), *Traffic* (2000), *21 Grams* (2004), *Syriana* (2006), and *Babel* (2006) (Bordwell 245–50).

6. In Richard R. John's thorough history of the development of telecommunication, *Network Nation* (2010), the transatlantic telephone line is a pivotal event. In his annual shareholders' report for 1910, Theodore N. Vail, the president of the American Telegraph and Telephone Company, announced an ambitious plan to consolidate the Bell telegraph and telephone lines into a "universal wire system" (340). That vision took a major step forward with the completion of the telephone line from New York to San Francisco in 1915, linking the

cluster of Bell lines in the East with those along the Pacific. Though the accomplishment only affected Bell patrons at first, the company's promise to make a "neighborhood of a nation" was powerful rhetoric matched by an equally powerful technological feat. There would not be a full integration of telephone and telegraph lines, however, due to antimonopoly legislation and lawsuits.

7. Castells writes that "multinational corporations are increasingly decentralized internal networks, organized in semi-autonomous units, according to countries, markets, processes, and products. Each one of these units links up with other semi-autonomous units of other multinationals, in the form of *ad hoc* strategic alliances. And each one of these alliances (in fact, networks) is a node of ancillary networks of small and medium firms" (122).

8. Berle and Means write: "No longer are the individuals in control of most of these companies, the dominant owners. Rather, there are no dominant owners, and control is maintained in large measure apart from ownership" (117).

9. Mizruchi's data show that intercorporation interlocks increased in number from 1904 to 1912 but declined from 1912 to 1935. He suggests that "what began around 1912 was a trend which would have occurred irrespective of the Clayton Act" (183). He explains the declining numbers by pointing to an accompanying decline of "heavily interlocked individuals" (184). In other words, as E. H. Harriman, John D. Rockefeller, J. P. Morgan Sr., and others—figures Josephson would label "robber barons"—died or reached retirement, the interlocking links between corporations often expired with them.

10. Of the legacy of the 1920s corporation, Didrichsen writes: "In the years which have passed since that decade, the strategy of diversification rather than that of integration, and the multidivisional as opposed to the functional organization have become dominant characteristics of many large firms in American industry" (38). The American corporation of the 1920s, in other words, is a signpost for the multinational corporate organization of Castells's study.

11. This seemingly arbitrary project of diversification motivates a running joke on NBC's sitcom *30 Rock* (2006–13), set mostly in the GE building on Rockefeller Plaza where NBC Studios are headquartered. GE executive Jack Donaghy (Alec Baldwin) carries the title of "Vice President of East Coast Television and Microwave Oven Programming" in the early seasons, when he often toggles schizophrenically between responsibilities managing a sketch comedy series and overseeing microwave product design. Later, he would be promoted to the head of NBC after it is taken over by the fictional outfit Kabletown—the series's parody of Comcast's acquisition of NBC Universal from GE in 2009.

12. For a startling visualization of the rise and fall of the United States rail

system, see Jean-Paul Rodrigue's chart "Rail Track Mileage and the Number of Class I Rail Carriers, United States, 1830–2012" at http://people.hofstra.edu/geotrans/eng/ch3en/conc3en/usrail18402003.html.

13. The electrical telegraph played a key role in coordinating military campaigns, with the Union operating some 15,000 miles of telegraph lines compared to the Confederacy's paltry 1,000 miles (John 101). And although President Lincoln had scoffed at the Pacific telegraph as late as 1859, he had changed his tune in the annual address to Congress in 1862, when he held that the electrical telegraph, steam power, and the rapid circulation of information had laid the groundwork for a single "national family"—a crucial bulwark against the two or more "families" proposed by the Confederacy (109). In other words, the distributive power of this technology was understood as a corrective for the disunion that was a stake in the Civil War and that had been a spectral possibility since the earliest days of the republic.

14. John writes that "the French optical telegraph relied on specially trained operators to relay coded messages along a chain of towers spaced at intervals of between 10 and 20 miles: the maximum distance by which an operator could interpret a signal using the telescopes of the day" (14). The term drew on the Greek roots for "writing-at-a-distance" and offered a reformulation of social space similar to the electrical device that would arrive in the 1840s bearing the same name (14).

15. *McClure's, Scribner's, Ladies' Home Journal, Smart Set, Collier's, Harper's*—these are but a sample of the venues that Mann argues "encouraged the popularity of stories and story cycles" during the modern period (8). Indeed, many stories from these cycles—Mann points to *Winesburg, Ohio, In Our Time,* and *The Unvanquished*—were first published in magazines and little magazines such as these.

16. See Moddelmog, "The Unifying Consciousness of a Divided Conscience."

17. See Leick, "Popular Modernism."

18. For a more expansive rehearsal of this argument, see Hegeman's *The Cultural Return* (2012), where the primary pressure on this "different historical relationship between the public and the private" is an emergent mass media (55).

19. See Smith, "Thread Structure"; see also Bordwell, "Subjective Stories and Network Narratives."

20. For Agamben, for example, totalization manifests in the singularity, which he describes in *The Coming Community* as "a being whose community

is mediated not by any condition of belonging (being red, being Italian, being Communist) nor by the simple absence of conditions (a negative community, such as that recently proposed in France by Maurice Blanchot), but by belonging itself" (85). Although singularity disclaims the false dilemma of the individual and the universal, for Agamben it also signals a "coming community" that is relatively smooth in its composition—especially because it repudiates the internal differentiation of identity categories.

Chapter 1

1. See, for instance, Gary Herstein's "The Roycean Roots of the Beloved Community." *The Pluralist* 4.2 (Summer 2009): 91–107.

2. Like Bourne, Kallen was interested in Jamesian pragmatism, and the two held a friendly disagreement over Bourne's critique of Dewey's support for the war. Likely in response to Bourne's June 1917 piece for *Seven Arts*, "War and the Intellectuals"—a bitter diatribe against the failures of pragmatism as it was bent to support the war effort—Kallen chided: "You do Dewey an injustice" before setting up a collegial meeting (Letter to Bourne).

3. "Federated" language informs the distributed logic of "Trans-National America" and also guides Bourne's thought in later essays. In "The War and the Intellectuals" (1917), Bourne laments the intellectual class's failure to investigate "a true Americanism which would not have been merely nebulous but might have federated the different ethnic groups and traditions" (5). In "From an Older Time" (1918), Bourne uses the term to discuss regionalism. He describes this project as "sectional but not separatist" and writes that its "federated picture would produce us a veritable American contemporary literature" (475)—a model similar to the program of Waldo Frank's *Our America* (1919).

4. "American transnationalism," Vaughan writes, "would begin where classical pluralism had left off: with the idea of democracy as a confederation—decentralized, pluralistic, self-critical, and self-correcting, in a Deweyan formulation of democracy that *creates* a public in the process and practice of democratic participation" (137).

5. An undated letter from Romains to a certain Figuière, perhaps an agent or a publisher, requests that Bourne be given copies of *Death of a Nobody* (1914) and *Power of Paris* (1911) for "a study to be presented in America."

6. Although Macdonald makes fair use of Bourne's material on mass culture, Bourne would have strenuously objected to the genealogy of Macdonald's jeremiad: "The turning point in our culture was the Civil War, whose aftermath

destroyed the New England tradition almost as completely as the October Revolution broke the continuity of Russian culture" (32). Indeed, it is hard to imagine anything more incongruous with Bourne's thesis than the praise of Brahmin New England as the center of purified American culture.

7. Of the young American's cosmopolitan ethic, Bourne writes: "If he is still a colonial, he is no longer the colonial of one partial culture, but of many. He is a colonial of the world. Colonialism has grown into cosmopolitanism" ("Trans-National" 118).

8. Susan Hegeman characterizes Frank's spatial-cultural diagramming as a schema "for imagining the transformation of American culture—from one of alienation and incompleteness to something approximating completion and organic integrity: what Frank himself liked to refer to as a 'Whole'" (*Patterns* 104).

Chapter 2

1. Close attention to Toomer's language in describing his objections to anthologizing excerpts of *Cane* reveals that another factor in those decisions could well have been his longstanding struggles with his own racial identity. In "This May Be Said / The Inside Story," he writes that he happily granted Countee Cullen's request to publish some of his poems but began to turn against the anthologies when he detected their New Negro agenda: "Soon," he writes, "I began seeing two things I did not like. I did not like the boosting and trumpeting and the over-play and over-valuation of the Negro, of the products of the Negro writers, which were springing up. I refused to have any part in this kind of displaying" (102). And he had serious trepidation about linking his own identity to the agenda of many of the black writers' anthologies: "I began discovering that the anthologies had preceded me. Not my own book *Cane*. No, but few people knew about *Cane*. Some, though, did know of the collections, and they had formed pictures and feelings about me based on their impressions of my work and name appearing in these collections" (103). It is no coincidence that this period, when he was losing his taste for requests to anthologize pieces from *Cane*, also corresponds to the period when Toomer began rejecting racial categorization of himself, refusing racial labels of "white" and "black" and choosing instead to be viewed as part of the "American race."

2. In this way, the strategy of "Beehive" resembles that of Claude McKay's "If We Must Die" (1919). Although McKay's sonnet retains a conventional rhyme scheme, there remains a sharp juxtaposition between its traditional, Eurocentric form and its content, which displays a radical and defiant dissent during the

Red Summer of 1919—situating McKay in a long history of black nationalism.

3. Goldberg contends that labor organizing created the upheaval in the South and not labor competition, which spurred the midsummer conflict in Chicago and which tends to get more attention in studies of the crisis. "Nothing disturbed southern whites more than the idea that African Americans might organize to demand their economic and political rights," Goldberg asserts (93). These fears manifested in the October 1919 riots at Elaine, Arkansas, where sharecroppers' establishment of the Progressive Farmers and Householders Union prompted a violent response by local whites (93).

4. See Rosalind Williams's "Jules Romains, *Unanimisme* and the Poetics of Urban Systems" (1992), which describes the materiality of Romains's philosophy in further detail.

5. In an oft-quoted letter from 1922, Toomer wrote to Anderson: "Winesburg, Ohio and The Triumph of the Egg are elements of my growing. It is hard to think of myself as maturing without them" (18). Toomer also dedicated "Kabnis," the third section of *Cane*, to Frank.

6. Note the epigraph's similarity to Toomer's concern that *Cane*, "which is an organism," might be "dismembered" by anthology editors.

7. For instance, see the 1923 study *Waldo Frank*, in which Gorham Munson suggests that *City Block* would establish an American school of unanimisme (53).

8. For the definitive historical records of Toomer's life, see the genealogical work commissioned and analyzed by Rudolph P. Byrd and Henry Louis Gates Jr. in "Jean Toomer's Racial Self-Identification: A Note on the Supporting Materials" in *Cane*, 2d ed. (New York: Norton, 2011), lxvi–lxxix.

9. David Goldberg explains that this version of the Klan billed itself as white supremacist while also "claiming to be 'the friend of the Negro.' As proof of its good intentions, the Klan made financial contributions to black churches" (125). Of course, despite such contributions, and despite the fact that the Klan's revival coincided with a decline in lynchings, the organization's very presence was understood as a marker of racial division, as demonstrated by the scorn African Americans heaped on the ministers who accepted such donations (118, 125).

10. In *Caribbean Discourse* (1981), Glissant writes: "What is the Caribbean, in fact? A multiple series of relationships" (139). In *Poetics of Relation* (1990), Glissant returns to antillanité and contrasts it with the hybrid figure of *créolité*: Caribbeanness "would link cultures across language barriers," whereas "the principles of creoleness regress toward negritudes, ideas of Frenchness, of Latinness, all generalizing concepts" (xxi, 89). Glissant describes the creole as "root identity" and antillanité as "Relation identity" (143–44).

Chapter 3

1. In a 1949 piece for the *New York Times*, Loos boasted of a *Blondes* comic strip as well as Lorelei-themed dress fabrics and wallpaper and even a song by Irving Berlin ("Musical" 59).

2. After he first met Loos, Huxley would write to his brother that "Miss Loos was ravishing. One would like to keep her for a pet" (Carey 189).

3. "A hotel's public spaces," Sandoval-Strausz writes, "were the heart and soul of the establishment: the places where people spent their time, the part observers said the most about, the areas of the liveliest sociability and innovation" (165).

4. According to Alexis Gregory, through the modern period bar sales were so crucial to hotels' business models that Prohibition consigned many to bankruptcy (27–28).

5. Sandoval-Strausz argues that hotels "created what might be called a multiplier effect: because people came to the same hotel spaces for many different reasons, there was constant crossing and commingling that exposed people to unexpected individuals and ideas. Someone who went to a hotel for a political caucus would also encounter travelers, their unfamiliar accents or foreign languages, and their styles of dress and comportment; by the same token, a person who ventured into a hotel for a shot of whiskey might thereby come into contact with antiliquor activists, itinerant physicians, society debutantes, or revivalist preachers. In short, hotels both focused and amplified the transformative power of human interaction" (261).

6. Noting another context of Lorelei's use of public spaces, Susan Hegeman writes that *Blondes* arrives in a moment when the workplace was becoming another site of public engagement: "growing numbers of women were finding it either desirable or necessary to find work outside the home. Though many kinds of factory work were being gradually closed to women, jobs as secretaries, file clerks, stenographers, and switchboard operators were plentiful, enticing young women like Lorelei into 'business colledges' across the country" ("Taking *Blondes* Seriously" 536).

7. Lorelei establishes the importance of this setting early on. In the third diary entry, she recalls having invited "all of the brainy gentlemen I could think up" the day before, only to awaken to wreckage that morning: "Heaven knows how long it will take to get the chandelier fixed" (*Blondes* 7). The very cryptic nature of the joke performs the blurring of boundaries of class and gender norms.

Chapter 4

1. For example, the British publisher of *The 42nd Parallel* wanted to eliminate altogether the Newsreels and Camera Eyes from its edition (Ludington 287).

2. Pizer writes that Dos Passos's letters "reveal that he conceived of and wrote each narrative as a single 'story,' and gave all his energy to this narrative until it was completed" (88).

3. Pizer's archival study finds that Dos Passos had in mind an elaborate "juxtapositional order of the modal segments" in mind even before he began drafting the discrete narrative modes: "His early division of each narrative into segments, and his attachment of specific biographical figures to specific narrative figures (Taylor to Ike Hall, for example), no doubt supplied him with a rough arrangement for this portion of the novel almost from the beginning of the compositional process" (88–89).

4. Pizer, I should note, pushes back on this critical metaphor, drawing on his study of the drafting process for *U.S.A.* "An analogy with assembly-line production, in which independently manufactured components are at last brought together," he writes, "inevitably comes to mind" (87). "Inevitably," but not decisively—Pizer ultimately dismisses it because his study refutes any assumption that the formal project was only accomplished at the very end of the process, but the Fordist analogy nevertheless retains a special appeal for describing the spatial logic of the text.

5. Kadlec writes that Vertov's influence on Dos Passos is certain: during his tour of Moscow and Leningrad in 1928, Dos Passos attended screenings of some of Vertov's "historical pictures," which he preferred to "the grander, state-backed productions of [Sergei] Eisenstein and Vsevolod Pudovkin" (307). However, Kadlec concludes that "the link between the two artists is finally superficial" because Dos Passos failed to heed Vertov's call for an art that would undermine the conventional distinctions between film, literature, and theater (307).

6. Nanney writes that in *Birth of a Nation* (1915) and *Intolerance* (1916) D. W. Griffith developed nearly all the montage techniques that would become common in American film through the Depression era and that would influence Dos Passos's stylistic and formal work. "Particularly applicable to Dos Passos's style," she writes, "are the techniques of continuity editing and of dramatic crosscutting" (142). Continuity editing creates a sense of ongoing motion by juxtaposing discontinuous images and as a consequence collapses narrative space and time apart from the total chronology of the work; crosscutting creates meaning through the juxtaposition of successive images (142). Equally

important to Dos Passos's work, Nanney continues, "was that Griffith used his techniques to create what he intended as epics of the American nation" (142). With its fragmentary rhythms of montage edits paired with the totalizing impulse of the epic, Griffith's work serves as an exemplar of the cultural logic of modernism.

7. See Christopher Phillips's introduction to *Montage and Modern Life, 1919–1942* (1992) for a more detailed genealogy of montage in the visual arts.

8. Donald Pizer describes this technique as "interlacing," and in his monograph on *U.S.A.* reproduces sketches by which Dos Passos mapped out character relations. Some of these sketches closely resemble the networked diagrams of today's data visualizations.

9. Although some figures cross over between *U.S.A.*'s four narrative modes—for example, Isadora Duncan is mentioned in Newsreel XIV in *The 42nd Parallel* and has a biographical profile in *The Big Money*—Bingham's newsreel publicity is confined to the fictional mode alone. The interplay of Bingham's appearance in a Pathé Newsreel and *U.S.A.*'s formal Newsreel element nevertheless demonstrates a point of repetition wherein Dos Passos's fiction reinforces his distributed narrative architecture.

10. The title not only invokes the culture industry but may be quite rooted in Dos Passos's experience within it. "It is perhaps not surprising," Denning writes, "that the phrase 'the big money' came out of Dos Passos's unhappy stint working in Hollywood during the summer of 1934" (*Cultural Front* 190).

11. See David Goldberg's *Discontented America* on capital's triumph over labor in the 1920s. Charley does not engage any of the union-busting strategies described by Goldberg, but he demonstrates the period's antagonism toward labor. When Bill Cermak relates workers' complaints that they are too overworked for sex and suggests that they consider unionizing the plant, Charley responds that the executives will simply "make 'em understand our problems"—offering not violence but a passive deferral of unionization and a complete dismissal of the workers' needs (Dos Passos, *Big Money* 249).

12. Sartre provides an anecdote of a queue at a bus stop to demonstrate seriality, which he describes as a state characterized by "a plurality of isolations" (*Critique* 256). No individual has a relation to another aside from the common need for transportation, and therefore each individual is interchangeable in the series. The series, then, is generally a "social product of cities" (257). Sartre's anecdote, as well as his conclusion, for seriality echoes the urban milieu of Romains's unanimisme.

13. "Historicism contents itself with establishing a causal connection

between various moments in history," Benjamin argues. "But no fact that is a cause is for that very reason historical. It became historical posthumously, as it were, through events that may be separated from it by thousands of years" ("Theses", 263).

14. The *District of Columbia* trilogy—*Adventures of a Young Man* (1938), *Number One* (1943), and *The Grand Design* (1949)—intersperses prose poems between the longer chapters of conventional, realist prose. But these act more as epigraphs and do not suggest an interplay of distributed narration. Likewise, *Chosen Country* (1951) also pares back *U.S.A.*'s formal experiment. Here instead of prose poems the narrative chapters are punctuated by portraits of Dos Passos's family and friends, substituting fictionalized renderings of his parents, members of his World War I ambulance group, and so on for *U.S.A.*'s great-men-of-history biographies. In both the *District of Columbia* and *Chosen Country*, the dynamic spatial movement of *U.S.A.*'s form is reduced to a more simple polarity.

15. Denning notes Dos Passos's tense relation to the postwar milieu, which relates equally to his changing politics and his steady investment in formalism: "to put it crudely, his move to the radical right lost him his left-wing admirers, while the undisputed sense that his early works are his finest made him a difficult icon for the right. . . . Unlike many of his contemporaries, he did not move from a radical political art to an apolitical formalism, and thus never won the allegiance of formalist or aestheticist critics" (*Cultural Front* 167).

Chapter 5

1. The man did not jump. Indeed, Galbraith finds no statistical evidence of a rise in suicides among New York traders after the crash, and speculates that the myth of the jumping trader was the work of sensationalist media (133, 135). Nevertheless, variations on the taunt "Jump!" appeared on signage outside the Stock Exchange during protests of the 2008 crash and the ensuing Troubled Asset Relief Program.

2. From the struggle between art and "the cheap clichés and disorder of mass culture," Barnard writes that art emerges victorious in these late modern studies of West's fiction. "The value of West's novels, in such readings," Barnard explains, "transcends and solves the problem of the vacuous and vicious culture represented in them" (10).

3. Hackwork did have its virtues. West told his friends that "he preferred to work on B or even C pictures, since writing these was mechanical and did not involve creative energy at all," according to Jay Martin (287). Martin describes

West's position as ambivalent: "he neither had illusions about the value of his screenplays nor felt that he had been exploited in doing them" (287).

4. Note the similarity to the conditions for a true common experience that Jean-Paul Sartre posits in *Critique of Dialectical Reason*: a group "makes itself into a community by feeling individual need as common need, and by projecting itself, in the internal unification of a common integration, towards objectives which it produces as common" (350).

5. Le Bon's proclamation of the crowded twentieth century was fairly commonplace. In *The Aesthetics and Politics of the Crowd in American Literature* (2003) Mary Esteve situates this position alongside Friedrich Nietzsche, who in *Beyond Good and Evil* (1886) referred to "the century of the crowd," and William James, whose preface to *The Principles of Psychology* (1890) characterized the turn of the century as "this crowded age" (2). Russ Castronovo, however, shows that progressive sociologists recognized the democratizing potential of crowds as well as their destructive, irrational capacities, pointing to the pioneering American sociologist Robert Park, whose 1904 dissertation "invests collective frenzy and rational public opinion equally with the potential of social transformation" (94–96).

6. Later thinkers would refuse judgment of the crowd's character while still retaining Le Bon's understanding of its composition. In his study of group formations in *Critique of Dialectical Reason*, for example, Jean-Paul Sartre describes the fused group as "an undifferentiated totality" in which action is performed "not as an individual, nor as an Other, but as an individual incarnation of the common person" (382, 357).

7. See Shepard's "Nathanael West Rewrites Horatio Alger, Jr.," *Satire Newsletter* 3.1 (1965), and Scharnhorst's "From Rags to Patches, or *A Cool Million* as Alter-Alger," *Ball State University Forum* 21.4 (1980). Also, for an argument against West's pastiche, see Aaron Talbot's "Fabricating the Fake Shoddy: Nathanael West's Parody of Horatio Alger, Jr." from his dissertation, "Peculiar Information, Partic'lar Friends: How American Literature and Culture Know Horatio Alger, Jr.," U of Florida, 2009.

8. For more on the political valences of the parade during the modern period, see Brooke L. Blower's remarkable study of the 1927 parade of the American Legionnaires through Paris in *Becoming Americans in Paris* (2011).

9. "All feeling and thoughts are bent in the direction by the hypnotizer," Le Bon writes. "Such is also approximately the state of the individual forming part of a psychological crowd. He is no longer conscious of his acts" (31).

10. "Early movie audiences could not be standardized, as they are today,"

Castronovo explains, "into the singular identity of an absorbed spectator but instead remained something much more uncertain and much less calculable: the crowd. Not only did films feature scenes of 'crowd splendor' and not only might crowds be dubbed a 'moving picture of democracy.'. . . Movies were not simply for or about crowds; this new art form might be productive of them" (142).

11. In a broader rendering of this argument in *The Cultural Return*, Hegeman keys in on the mass media as a particular culprit in the phenomenon of atomization, especially in the event at Asbury Park. Not only did mass media attract the crowds to the shoreline, but they also broadcast to listeners on foreign continents the bizarre and at times grotesque atmosphere at the beach. But for Hegeman, this crowd is still more distinct among its modern peers: "this incident, where production and consumption are conspicuously intermingled through the presence of an actively participatory crowd, violates a conventional definition of mass media, which emphasizes the spatial and temporal separation of mass media producers and consumers" (48). It is no coincidence that it is the radio again—that hallmark of modern distribution—that plays a major role in this narrative: even as it appears to consolidate the onlookers into an undifferentiated mass, the radio's ultimate achievement is the mediation of a constellar social space.

Works Cited

Agamben, Giorgio. *The Coming Community*. 1990. Trans. Michael Hardt. Minneapolis: U Minnesota P, 1993. Theory Out of Bounds 1.

Barnard, Rita. *The Great Depression and the Culture of Abundance: Kenneth Fearing, Nathanael West, and Mass Culture in the 1930s*. New York: Cambridge UP, 1995.

Barreca, Regina. Introduction. *Gentlemen Prefer Blondes: The Illuminating Diary of a Professional Lady* and *But Gentlemen Marry Brunettes*. By Anita Loos. Illus. Ralph Barton. New York: Penguin, 1998. vii–xxiv.

Benjamin, Walter. *The Arcades Project*. 1982. Trans. Howard Eiland and Kevin McLaughlin. Ed. Rolf Tiedemann. Cambridge, MA: Belknap Press of Harvard UP, 2004.

———. "Theses on the Philosophy of History." 1950. *Illuminations*. Trans. Harry Zohn. Ed. Hannah Arendt. New York: Schocken Books, 1969. 253–64.

Berle, Adolf, and Gardiner Means. *The Modern Corporation and Private Property*. 1932. New York: Macmillan, 1937.

Blake, Casey Nelson. *Beloved Community: The Cultural Criticism of Randolph Bourne, Van Wyck Brooks, Waldo Frank, and Lewis Mumford*. Chapel Hill: U of North Carolina P, 1990.

Bordwell, David. "Mutual Friends and Chronologies of Chance." *Poetics of Cinema*. New York: Routledge, 2008. 189–250.

———. "Subjective Stories and Network Narratives." *The Way Hollywood Tells It*. Berkeley: U California P, 2006. 72–103.

Bourne, Randolph. "Americanism." 1916. *New Republic* 23 September 1916: 197.

———. "From an Older Time." 1918. *The Radical Will: Selected Writings, 1911–1918*. Ed. Olaf Hansen. Berkeley: U California P, 1977. 475–79.

———. "The Jew and Trans-National America." 1916. *War and the Intellectuals: Collected Essays, 1915–1919*. Ed. Carl Resek. Indianapolis: Hackett, 1999. 124–33.

———. Letter to Alyse Gregory. 5 July 1914. TS. Randolph Bourne Papers. Columbia University Rare Book and Manuscript Lib., New York.

———. "Old Tyrannies." 1919. *The Radical Will: Selected Writings, 1911–1918*. Ed. Olaf Hansen. Berkeley: U California P, 1977. 169–73.
———. "Pageantry and Social Art." *The Radical Will: Selected Writings, 1911–1918*. Ed. Olaf Hansen. Berkeley: U California P, 1977. 515–19.
———. "A Sociological Poet." *The Radical Will: Selected Writings, 1911–1918*. Ed. Olaf Hansen. Berkeley: U California P, 1977. 520–27.
———. "Trans-National America." 1916. *War and the Intellectuals: Collected Essays, 1915–1919*. Ed. Carl Resek. Indianapolis: Hackett, 1999. 107–23.
———. "The War and the Intellectuals." 1917. *War and the Intellectuals: Collected Essays, 1915–1919*. Ed. Carl Resek. Indianapolis: Hackett, 1999. 3–14.
Bridgman, Richard. *Gertrude Stein in Pieces*. New York: Oxford UP, 1970.
Byrd, Rudolph P., and Henry Louis Gates Jr. "'Song of the Son': The Emergence and Passing of Jean Toomer." *Cane*. By Jean Toomer. Ed. Rudolph P. Byrd and Henry Louis Gates Jr. 2d ed. Norton Critical Editions. New York: Norton, 2011. xix–lxvi.
Carey, Gary. *Anita Loos: A Biography*. New York: Knopf, 1988.
Castells, Manuel. *The Rise of the Network Society*. 1996. 2d ed. Malden, MA: Blackwell, 2000.
Castronovo, Russ. *Beautiful Democracy: Aesthetics and Anarchy in a Global Era*. Chicago: U Chicago P, 2007.
Churchwell, Sarah. "'Lost Among the Ads': *Gentlemen Prefer Blondes* and the Politics of Imitation." *Middlebrow Moderns: Popular American Writers of the 1920s*. Ed. Lisa Botshon and Meredith Goldsmith. Boston: Northeastern UP, 2003. 135–64.
Ciccoricco, David. *Reading Network Fiction*. Tuscaloosa: U Alabama P, 2007.
Clayton, Bruce. *Forgotten Prophet: The Life of Randolph Bourne*. Baton Rouge: Louisiana State UP, 1984.
The Crowd. Dir. King Vidor. Perf. Eleanor Boardman, James Murray. 1928. VHS. Warner Home Video, 1998.
Dash, J. Michael. *Edouard Glissant*. New York: Cambridge UP, 1995. Cambridge Studies in African and Caribbean Literature.
Denning, Michael. *The Cultural Front: The Laboring of American Culture in the Twentieth Century*. 1997. New York: Verso, 1998.
———. *Culture in the Age of Three Worlds*. New York: Verso, 2004.
Didrichsen, Jon. "The Development of Diversified and Conglomerate Firms in the United States, 1920–1970." 1972. *Men and Organizations: The American Economy in the Twentieth Century*. Ed. Edwin J. Perkins. New York: Putnam's, 1977. 38–50.

Dixon, Royal. *Americanization*. New York: Macmillan, 1916.
Dos Passos, John. *The 42nd Parallel*. 1930. New York: Mariner, 2000.
———. *1919*. 1932. New York: Mariner, 2000.
———. *The Big Money*. 1936. New York: Mariner, 2000.
Dunn, Maggie, and Ann Morris. *The Composite Novel: The Short Story Cycle in Transition*. New York: Twayne, 1995.
Esteve, Mary. *The Aesthetics and Politics of the Crowd in American Literature*. New York: Cambridge UP, 2003.
"Fiction, But Not Novels." Rev. of *Three Lives*, by Gertrude Stein. *Kansas City Star* 18 December 1909. Rpt. in *The Critical Response to Gertrude Stein*. Ed. Kirk Curnutt. Westport, CT: Greenwood, 2000: 10.
Ford, Karen Jackson. *Split-Gut Song: Jean Toomer and the Poetics of Modernity*. Tuscaloosa: U Alabama P, 2005.
Frank, Waldo. *City Block*. Darien, CT: Waldo Frank, 1922.
———. *Our America*. New York: Boni and Liverwright, 1919.
"A Futurist Novel." Rev. of *Three Lives*, by Gertrude Stein. *Philadelphia Public Ledger* 10 April 1915. Rpt. in *The Critical Response to Gertrude Stein*. Ed. Kirk Curnutt. Westport, CT: Greenwood, 2000: 12–13.
Galbraith, John Kenneth. *The Great Crash, 1929*. 1954. Boston: Houghton Mifflin, 1972.
Galloway, Alexander R., and Eugene Thacker. *The Exploit: A Theory of Networks*. Minneapolis: U Minnesota P, 2007.
Glissant, Edouard. *Caribbean Discourse: Selected Essays*. 1981. Trans. J. Michael Dash. Charlottesville: U Virginia P, 1989. Caraf Books.
———. *Poetics of Relation*. 1990. Trans. Betsy Wing. Ann Arbor: U Michigan P, 1997.
Goldberg, David J. *Discontented America: The United States in the 1920s*. Baltimore: Johns Hopkins UP, 1999.
Grand Hotel. Dir. Edmund Goulding. Perf. Greta Garbo, John Barrymore, Joan Crawford. 1932. Warner Brothers, 2008. DVD.
Gregory, Alexis. "U.S.A.: Size and Fantasy." *Grand American Hotels*. New York: Vendome, 1989. 11–37.
Hardt, Michael, and Antonio Negri. *Commonwealth*. Cambridge: The Belknap Press of Harvard UP, 2009.
———. *Multitude: War and Democracy in the Age of Empire*. New York: Penguin, 2004.
Hegeman, Susan. *The Cultural Return*. Berkeley: U of California P, 2012.
———. "Haunted by Mass Culture." *American Literary History* 12.1–2 (2000):

298–317.
———. *Patterns for America: Modernism and the Concept of Culture*. Princeton: Princeton UP, 1999.
———. "Taking *Blondes* Seriously." *American Literary History* 7.3 (Autumn 1995): 525–54.
Hobhouse, Janet. *Everybody Who Was Anybody: A Biography of Gertrude Stein*. 1975. New York: Anchor, 1989.
Ingram, Forrest L. *Representative Short Story Cycles of the Twentieth Century: Studies in a Literary Genre*. The Hague: Mouton, 1971.
Irr, Caren. *The Suburb of Dissent: Cultural Politics in the United States and Canada during the 1930s*. Durham, NC: Duke UP, 1998.
James, Henry. *The American Scene*. 1907. New York: St. Martin's, 1987.
Jameson, Fredric. *A Singular Modernity: Essay on the Ontology of the Present*. New York: Verso, 2002.
John, Richard R. *Network Nation: Inventing American Telecommunications*. Cambridge: Belknap Press of Harvard UP, 2010.
Josephson, Matthew. *The Robber Barons: The Great American Capitalists, 1861–1901*. New York: Harcourt, Brace, 1934.
Kadlec, David. "Early Soviet Cinema and American Poetry." *Modernism/modernity* 11.2 (2004): 299–331.
Kallen, Horace. "Democracy Versus the Melting-Pot: A Study of American Nationality." 1915. *Nation*, pt. 1, 18 February 1915: 190–94; pt. 2, 25 February 1915: 217–20.
———. Letter to Randolph Bourne. 25 August 1917. TS. Randolph Bourne Papers. Columbia University Rare Book and Manuscript Lib., New York.
Kazin, Alfred. *On Native Grounds: An Interpretation of Modern American Prose Literature*. 1942. New York: Harvest, 1995. 312–59.
Kellor, Frances A. *Straight America: A Call to National Service*. New York: Macmillan, 1916.
Kennedy, J. Gerald. "Introduction: The American Short Story Sequence—Definitions and Implications." *Modern American Short Story Sequences: Composite Fictions and Fictive Communities*. Ed. J. Gerald Kennedy. New York: Cambridge UP, 1995. vii–xv.
Koolhaas, Rem. *Delirious New York: A Retroactive Manifesto for Manhattan*. 1978. New York: Monacelli, 1994.
Larson, Edward J. *Summer for the Gods: The Scopes Trial and America's Continuing Debate over Science and Religion*. 1997. New York: Basic, 2006.
Le Bon, Gustave. *The Crowd: A Study of the Popular Mind*. 1895. New York:

Viking, 1960.

LeClair, Mark S. *International Commodity Markets and the Role of Cartels.* Armonk, NY: M. E. Sharpe, 2000.

Leick, Karen. "Popular Modernism: Little Magazines and the American Daily Press." *PMLA* 123.1 (January 2008): 125–39.

Loos, Anita. "The Biography of a Book." 1963. *Fate Keeps on Happening: Adventures of Lorelei Lee and Other Writings.* Ed. Ray Pierre Corsini. New York: Dodd, Mead, 1984. 53–61.

———. *But Gentlemen Marry Brunettes.* 1928. *Gentlemen Prefer Blondes: The Illuminating Diary of a Professional Lady and But Gentlemen Marry Brunettes.* Illus. Ralph Barton. New York: Penguin, 1998. 125–243.

———. "Cocktail Parties of the Twenties." 1970. *Fate Keeps on Happening: Adventures of Lorelei Lee and Other Writings.* Ed. Ray Pierre Corsini. New York: Dodd, Mead, 1984. 95–99.

———. *Gentlemen Prefer Blondes: The Illuminating Diary of a Professional Lady.* 1925. *Gentlemen Prefer Blondes: The Illuminating Diary of a Professional Lady* and *But Gentlemen Marry Brunettes.* Illus. Ralph Barton. New York: Penguin, 1998. 1–123.

———. "A Musical Is Born." 1949. *Fate Keeps on Happening: Adventures of Lorelei Lee and Other Writings.* Ed. Ray Pierre Corsini. New York: Dodd, Mead, 1984. 58–61.

Ludington, Townsend. *John Dos Passos: A Twentieth-Century Odyssey.* New York: Dutton, 1980.

Macdonald, Dwight. "Masscult and Midcult." 1960. *Masscult and Midcult: Essays Against the American Grain.* Ed. John Summers. New York: New York Review of Books, 2011. 3–71.

Mann, Susan Garland. *The Short Story Cycle: A Genre Companion and Reference Guide.* New York: Greenwood, 1989.

Martin, Jay. *Nathanael West: The Art of His Life.* New York: Farrar, Straus, and Giroux, 1970.

McGurl, Mark. *The Novel Art: Elevations of American Fiction after Henry James.* Princeton: Princeton UP, 2001.

Mencken, H. L. "The Sahara of the Bozart." 1920. *A Mencken Chrestomathy.* Ed. H. L. Mencken. New York: Knopf, 1949. 184–95.

Mills, Nicolaus. *The Crowd in American Literature.* Baton Rouge: Louisiana State UP, 1986.

Mizruchi, Mark. *The American Corporate Network, 1904–1974.* Beverly Hills, CA: Sage, 1982. Sage Library of Social Research 138.

Moddelmog, Debra. "The Unifying Consciousness of a Divided Conscience: Nick Adams as Author of *In Our Time*." *American Literature* 60.4 (December 1988): 591–610.
Montgomery-Massingberd, Hugh. "A Homage to César Ritz." *Grand Hotel: The Golden Age of Palace Hotels; an Architectural and Social History*. New York: Vendome, 1984. 147–53.
Munson, Gorham. *Waldo Frank: A Study*. New York: Boni and Liveright, 1923.
Nanney, Lisa. *John Dos Passos Revisited*. New York: Twayne, 1998. Twayne's United States Author Series 700.
Nasaw, David. *Going Out: The Rise and Fall of Public Amusements*. New York: Basic, 1993.
North, Michael. *The Dialect of Modernism: Race, Language, and Twentieth-Century Literature*. New York: Oxford UP, 1994.
Peckham, Joel B. "Jean Toomer's *Cane*: Self as Montage and the Drive toward Integration." *American Literature* 72.2 (June 2000): 275–90.
Perloff, Marjorie. "The Invention of Collage." *Collage*. Ed. Jeanine Parisier Plottel. New York: New York Literary Forum, 1983. 5–47.
Phillips, Christopher. Introduction. *Montage and Modern Life, 1919–1942*. Ed. Matthew Teitelbaum. Cambridge, MA: MIT Press, 1992. 20–35.
Pizer, Donald. *Dos Passos' U.S.A.: A Critical Study*. Charlottesville: UP of Virginia, 1988.
Posnock, Ross. "The Politics of Nonidentity: A Genealogy." *boundary 2* 19.1 (Spring 1992): 34–68.
Romains, Jules. Letter to Figuière. N.d. MS. Randolph Bourne Papers. Columbia University Rare Book and Manuscript Lib., New York.
Roth, Henry. *Call It Sleep*. 1934. New York: Picador, 1991.
Rudel, Anthony. *Hello, Everybody!: The Dawn of American Radio*. New York: Harcourt, 2008.
Sandoval-Strausz, A. K. *Hotel: An American History*. New Haven, CT: Yale UP, 2007.
Sartre, Jean-Paul. *Critique of Dialectical Reason, Volume One: Theory of Practical Ensembles*. 1960. Trans. Alan Sheridan-Smith. Ed. Jonathan Rée. New York: Verso, 2004.
———. "John Dos Passos and *1919*." 1947. *Literary and Philosophical Essays*. Trans. Annette Michelson. New York: Criterion, 1955. 88–96.
Scruggs, Charles, and Lee VanDemarr. *Jean Toomer and the Terrors of American History*. Philadelphia: U Pennsylvania P, 1998.
Seguin, Robert. *Around Quitting Time: Work and Middle-Class Fantasy in*

American Fiction. Durham, NC: Duke UP, 2001.
Siegel, Robert, and Melissa Block. "At Least Three People Killed in Boston Attack." National Public Radio, 15 April 2013. Web. 17 April 2013.
Smith, Evan. "Thread Structure: Rewriting the Hollywood Formula." *Journal of Film and Video* 51.3–4 (Fall–Winter 1999): 88–96.
Souhami, Diana. *Gertrude and Alice*. London: Phoenix, 1991.
Springer, John Parris. *Hollywood Fictions: The Dream Factory in American Popular Literature*. Norman: U Oklahoma P, 2000.
Stansell, Christine. *American Moderns: Bohemian New York and the Creation of a New Century*. New York: Henry Holt, 2000.
Stein, Gertrude. *Three Lives: Stories of the Good Anna, Melanctha, and the Gentle Lena*. 1909. Mansfield Centre, CT: Martino, 2012.
Thomas, Jean-Jacques. "Collage/Space/Montage." *Collage*. Ed. Jeanine Parisier Plottel. New York: New York Literary Forum, 1983. 79–102.
Tichi, Cecelia. *Shifting Gears: Technology, Literature, Culture in Modernist America*. Chapel Hill: U North Carolina P, 1987. 194–216.
Toomer, Jean. *Cane*. 1923. Ed. Darwin T. Turner. Norton Critical Editions. New York: Norton, 1988. 1–117.
———. "This May Be Said / The Inside Story." [c. 1932.] *A Jean Toomer Reader: Selected Unpublished Writings*. Ed. Frederik L. Rusch. New York: Oxford UP, 1993. 101–04.
———. "To Sherwood Anderson." 18 December 1922. *A Jean Toomer Reader: Selected Unpublished Writings*. Ed. Frederik L. Rusch. New York: Oxford UP, 1993. 17–18.
Trachtenberg, Alan. *The Incorporation of America: Culture and Society in the Gilded Age*. 1982. New York: Hill and Wang, 1994.
Van Vechten, Carl. Introduction. *Three Lives*. By Gertrude Stein. New York: Modern Library, 1933. v–xi.
Vaughan, Leslie J. *Randolph Bourne and the Politics of Cultural Radicalism*. Lawrence: UP of Kansas, 1997.
West, Nathanael. *A Cool Million: The Dismantling of Lemuel Pitkin*. 1934. *Nathanael West: Novels and Other Writings*. Ed. Sacvan Bercovitch. New York: Library of America, 1997. 127–238.
———. *The Day of the Locust*. 1939. New York: Signet, 1983.
———. *Miss Lonelyhearts*. 1933. *Miss Lonelyhearts and The Day of the Locust*. New York: New Directions, 1962. 1–58.
Whalan, Mark. *Race, Manhood, and Modernism in America: The Short Story Cycles of Sherwood Anderson and Jean Toomer*. Knoxville: U Tennessee P, 2007.

Williams, Rosalind. "Jules Romains, *Unanimisme*, and the Poetics of Urban Systems." *Literature and Technology*. Ed. Mark L. Greenberg and Lance Schachterle. Bethlehem, PA: Lehigh UP, 1992. Research in Technology Studies 5. 177–205.

Williamson, Jefferson. *The American Hotel: An Anecdotal History*. New York: Knopf, 1930.

Index